Surviving the Mob

A Street Soldier's Life Inside the Gambino Crime Family

Dennis N. Griffin
and Andrew DiDonato

Huntington Press
Las Vegas Nevada

Surviving the Mob
A Street Soldier's Life Inside the Gambino Crime Family

Published by
Huntington Press
3665 Procyon St.
Las Vegas, NV 89103
Phone (702) 252-0655
e-mail: books@huntingtonpress.com

ISBN: 978-1-935396-38-3
Library of Congress Control Number: 2010934074
$14.95US

Cover Photos: Brooklyn Bridge & Lower Manhattan skyline ©Mario Savoia/Dreamstime.com; Blood Paper ©ctvvele/Dreamstime.com
Photo Insert Pages: Background, Vintage Postcard ©Mikle15/Dreamstimes.com; Courtesy of Andrew DiDonato, pgs. 1, 2, 3, 9, 10 top, and 12; Courtesy of Billy Cutolo, Jr., pg. 4 top; Internet photos, pgs. 4 bottom, 5 top, 6 bottom, 7 bottom, and 8 top; Courtesy of NYPD, pgs. 5 bottom, 7 top, 8 bottom, 10 bottom, and 11; Courtesy of New York Daily News, pgs. 6 top

Production & Design: Laurie Cabot

Surviving the Mob

Dedication

This book is dedicated to the three most important people in my life. To my wife Lupe, whose love, kindness, and support have made me into a better person in so many ways. And to my daughter Mia, who has brought me happiness beyond anything I could ever have dreamed of.

And especially to my son Andrew, whom I love and miss more than words can say. The choices I made early in my life didn't allow me to be there for him as I should have been. I will regret those decisions for the rest of my life. My greatest hope is that through the pages of this book, he will find the long-awaited answers to his questions and come to know who I really am.

Andrew DiDonato

Acknowledgments

The information in this book was derived from a variety of sources, but primarily from Andrew DiDonato himself. However, many other resources provided valuable information to this project, including the *New York Post, New York Times, New York Daily News, Jerry Capeci's Gang Land News, Mafia Today, Mafia News Today,* and the websites of the FBI and the United States Department of Justice.

I also want to extend my special thanks to William Cutolo Jr. for his contribution to the discussion of the murder of his father, William "Wild Bill" Cutolo.

Several other people deserve mention, but due to their unique situations or for other reasons, they desire to stay in the background. Respecting their wishes, they will remain nameless, but not unappreciated.

Denny Griffin

Contents

Prologue

In the summer of 2009, I received an email from a lady who said she had a friend—an erstwhile mobster—who had a story to tell. She said if I was interested to give her a call. I did.

During my conversation with the woman, I was told that her friend was a former associate—a street soldier—of the Gambino crime family out of New York City. In 1997 he flipped and became a government witness. He testified at several high-profile Mob trials, including John Gotti Junior's.

Although he voluntarily left the federal Witness Protection Program, he was still an active witness, who would more than likely have to testify in pending cases. Therefore, his security was an issue. She would only identify him as Andrew. If I wanted to speak with him by phone, she would arrange it. After contemplating her offer for a couple of days, I asked her to put me in touch with him.

Over the next several days, I communicated with Andrew by phone and email. I learned that his last name was DiDonato. He was born in New York City in 1965 into a Mob-connected family. He had been involved in organized crime since he was a teen. His extensive criminal history included everything from illegal gambling to burglary, armed robbery, attempted murder and conspiracy to commit murder. He had served several years in state and federal prisons.

Andrew explained that he had reached out to me because of my previous Mob biography, *Cullotta*. Trust was a major issue with him, and he felt I had proved myself—made my bones, if you will—by co-authoring that book with the one-time Chicago Outfit-connected Frank Cullotta.

Andrew said his goal was to tell the story of life as an associate of an organized-crime family from a street soldier's perspective. He wanted to show it isn't the glamorous lifestyle many people think it is, and that when you're a criminal your actions hurt a lot of people, physically, emotionally, and financially.

I was intrigued by the project, but there was one very important issue that needed to be put to rest before I committed to helping Andrew with his book. I told him that I wouldn't get involved unless I was sure he would be totally candid and that the book would be factually accurate.

He said we both desired the same things: candor and accuracy. Much of the information he planned to disclose had been verified by law enforcement as part of his deal with the government. Events were also documented in newspaper articles and public records. He would only hold back any information that could impact future legal action against former colleagues in which he may have to testify. Andrew's answer satisfied me that we were on the same page and he began providing me with documents, articles, photos, and sites where I could find information.

Andrew and I finally met in person in December 2009. In January 2010 we began writing *Surviving the Mob*.

In these pages you'll read extensively about the Gambino crime family. The organization has had many notable bosses over the years, including Carlo Gambino, Paul Castellano, and John Gotti. However, here, the primary focus is on the capo of Andrew's crew, Nicholas "Nicky" Corozzo.

Nicky Corozzo was born in Brooklyn, New York, on

March 17, 1940. He was one of John Gotti's chief rivals within the family in the 1980s and rose in power after Gotti's incarceration in 1992. In 2005, Nicky was recognized by law enforcement as the boss of the Gambinos. So although he may lack the name recognition of some of his predecessors, Nicky Corozzo was a force to be reckoned with in New York organized crime.

After you've read this book, you'll have a much better understanding of how an organized-crime crew functions. You'll know what types of crimes they commit to make their money and how the proceeds are distributed. You'll learn about Mob politics and myths, that loyalty goes from the bottom up, but not necessarily from the top down. You'll experience Andrew's life on the run from the law, while also being under a death sentence from his former colleagues. And you'll get a taste of what it's like to do prison time and to be a government witness.

Denny Griffin
Las Vegas, January 2010

Introduction

My name is Andrew DiDonato. I was born on November 21, 1965, in Queens, New York. I was raised in Brooklyn in a house between two Mafia social clubs. I grew up under the watchful eyes of the neighborhood wiseguys.

My great-uncle Pasquale "Paddy Mac" Macchiarole was a capo in the Genovese family. When I was 12, Paddy was murdered in a Mob hit. Two months later, his son John was also killed gangland-style. I suppose that being exposed to that kind of violence at such a young age could or should have discouraged me from wanting to live the Mafia life. But it didn't. Maybe it was my destiny to become a criminal.

In 1979 at the age of 14, I started down that road. I began by stealing radios, tires, and wheels from cars with other neighborhood kids—some of whom later became affiliated with the same Gambino crew I did.

Over the next several months, I added shaking down drug dealers, selling marijuana, and stealing cars to my criminal activities. For a 15-year-old kid, I was making pretty good money.

But my big break in moving up the crime ladder came in 1982. A friend and I got arrested for assault and extortion. You might ask why I say getting busted was a big break. The answer is simple: It brought me to the attention of the criminal powers that be. It showed that I was serious and ambitious, a young guy with nerve and earning potential. These were all qualities the crime bosses looked for when taking on new blood. My arrest opened the door into the world of organized crime.

For the next 15 years, I was a Gambino street soldier. But I committed crimes with guys from the other New York families too: loansharking, bookmaking, assault, burglary, robbery, bank robbery, counterfeiting, attempted murder, and conspiracy to commit murder. I know now that the things I did hurt a lot of people. But I didn't realize it then.

The event that eventually led to my second chance in life came in 1996. A friend and I robbed a drug dealer associated with another crime family of $200,000. The repercussions from that score cost the lives of two people and nearly started a Mob war. They also caused me to become a fugitive from justice for 17 months and a target of my own crew and another family. It was during this time I began to see the Mob for what it really is. I became a cooperating government witness in 1997 and am still active in that capacity today. I'm lucky to be alive and I know it.

I'm telling my story not to make myself a hero or glamorize organized crime. On the contrary, I did a lot of bad stuff and nothing I do now can change that. This book isn't an apology or an appeal for sympathy. It's an explanation. It's my chance to lay it all out there and let you see what life as a Mob associate is like from the inside. After you've read it, you can reach your own conclusions.

Andrew DiDonato
October 2010

1

A Near-Death Experience

At approximately 1:50 on the afternoon of April 8, 1988, an elderly woman named Sandra Raiola was walking on East 2nd Street between Avenues O and P in Brooklyn, New York. This was a residential neighborhood that tended to be relatively peaceful and quiet.

As Sandra walked, she passed two men standing on the sidewalk arguing. A vehicle occupied by a driver was double-parked on the street next to the men. When Sandra neared the corner of Avenue P, she heard a popping noise from behind her, like a car backfiring or a firecracker exploding. She turned around and looked down the street in the direction of the noise. She saw one of the two men who had been arguing lying prone on the sidewalk, screaming, "Help me!" The other man was squatting next to him. Noticing her, the squatting man sprang to his feet and got into the double-parked vehicle. The car then sped past her, ran the red light at the corner of Avenue P, and quickly disappeared from view down East 2nd Street.

Sandra didn't know it at the time, but her presence at that location accomplished two very important things. First, it saved the life of the downed man, Ralph Burzo. Second, by doing so, it prevented the other man from becoming a murderer.

Burzo's assailant was Andrew DiDonato. He had already fired one round from his handgun into Burzo's head. It was Burzo's good fortune that the bullet struck a bone and splintered, causing serious, but not fatal, injuries. After his victim had fallen to the sidewalk, Andrew squatted next to him to administer a second life-ending shot. But before he could pull the trigger, he noticed Raiola watching him and fled the scene.

However, Andrew's escape was only temporary. He was arrested a short time later and on May 17, 1988, he was indicted by a Kings County Grand Jury for one count of attempted murder in the second degree, two counts of assault in the first degree, one count of criminal possession of a weapon in the second degree, and one count of criminal possession of a weapon in the third degree.

Samuel Karkis, the driver of the getaway car, was indicted on the same charges, plus hindering prosecution in the second degree.

The above account of events was taken primarily from that indictment and relates the facts of what took place. But it doesn't tell the story. It doesn't reveal the circumstances that brought Ralph Burzo, Samuel Karkis, and Andrew DiDonato to East 2nd Street near Avenue P that May afternoon. And it doesn't explain why Andrew wanted Burzo dead.

The story behind the shooting can't be addressed in a few sentences or paragraphs. In order to truly understand what happened that day and why, we have to go back out on the streets of Brooklyn nearly a decade before Andrew pulled the trigger.

Learning the Trade

In 1980, Andrew DiDonato was living with his mother and stepfather on East 55th Street in Brooklyn. At that time the minimum wage in the United States was $3.10 per hour. Assuming a 14- or 15-year-old boy like Andrew could get a job flipping burgers 20 hours a week after school, he'd gross $62 for his labor. Although Andrew worked when he wasn't in school, he didn't toil in a hamburger stand or anything similar. He did his work on the streets, and his weekly income was sometimes in the neighborhood of $1,400 cash. How did a kid his age generate that kind of money? As Andrew explains, it took hard work and nerve.

"I had two main sources of income in those days. I stole and sold car parts. And I shook down the kids selling marijuana in the neighborhood. I told them they'd either pay me a couple hundred bucks a week or I'd break their head."

Andrew knew that if you wanted to be respected on the sidewalks of Brooklyn, you couldn't just talk the talk. Out there, actions truly spoke louder than words and verbal threats alone weren't enough to prove you were a force to be reckoned with. That was a lesson of the streets Andrew learned early. And he learned it well.

"The killings of my uncle and cousin devastated my family. It was the first taste of the reality of how brutal that life can be. Although I didn't realize it at the time, it was a lesson that ultimately saved my life many years later."

Andrew's own capacity for violence became obvious as he advanced his extortion plans.

"Shaking down the pot dealers, I began with an act of violence, like a severe beating or a few shots with a baseball bat. I let them know there was worse to come if my demands weren't met."

Andrew wasn't physically imposing. He stood three inches or so under six feet and weighed around 160 pounds. Some of the dealers he wanted to move in on were bigger than he was and some were as tough, maybe even tougher. But that didn't deter him. He was thin and athletic and to overcome deficiencies in size or strength, he used the element of surprise to get the upper hand on his victim.

"I'd sneak up behind the guy and whack him with a bat. When he went down, I'd hit him again to make my point. They knew then I had something most of them didn't. I had the balls to do whatever it took to impose my will. So it really didn't matter if they were bigger than me. They knew if they fucked around with me, I'd get 'em with my fists, or a bat, or a tire iron. And they'd never even know it was coming. They were afraid of me and that's the way I wanted it."

Did Andrew ever feel guilty about the beatings he administered?

"I knew most of these dealers from school or the neighborhood. Some of them I didn't like and enjoyed beating up. But I wasn't just a bully. I was liked in the neighborhood and gave respect to those who deserved it. This was business, though, and I had to rough up the ones I liked, too. I was making a statement that if you were into selling weed, I wasn't playing favorites."

Andrew's tactics worked. In addition to the dealers falling into line, word circulated that a new kid out there needed to be taken seriously. In fairly short order, he had most of the young marijuana dealers in Bergen Beach paying him a street tax.

Extorting the dealers was primarily a one-man operation for Andrew. But stealing car parts, he often worked with other neighborhood youths.

"Some of the kids I stole with were already associated with organized-crime crews and several more of us got involved later. I made many good friends back then and I thought we'd be friends for life. But shit happens and in some cases, it didn't work out that way. And some of those I was closest with died before their time."

In those early days, Andrew and his buddies weren't proficient at stealing whole cars. Instead, they robbed parts.

For example, Mercedes Benz used Becker digital radios. They were a hot item. The thieves smashed in a window, ripped out the radio, and ran. Andrew's next-door neighbor, Rocco Corozzo, nephew of Gambino capo and Andrew's future boss Nicholas Corozzo, had a buyer for the radios who took all they brought him and paid between $150 and $200 a set.

"We were having fun and the guys in the street crews left us alone. We were just kids and they didn't make us kick anything in to them. Whatever we made was ours. It was all coming in and nothing had to be paid out."

But even criminals like Andrew can experience economic tough times. In the case of him and his friends, youth, inexperience, and greed were contributing factors, as well as unanticipated business interruptions.

"Sometimes when we had a lot of money in our pockets, we got a little lazy. We stopped stealing for a while and blew what we had buying stuff and partying. We were young and weren't thinking about saving. When we realized we were almost out of cash, we got off our asses and went back to work.

"I even screwed myself by taking so much from the dealers I was shaking down that I put some of them out of business. By the time they made their payment to me and bought product, they weren't making enough profit to stay in business. When one of 'em went away, it might be a few weeks before someone stepped in to take his place and I could get to the new guy to explain the cost of doing business.

"And then there were supply interruptions. When the dealers didn't have anything to sell, they weren't making any money and they weren't paying me. Depending on the reason for the interruption, it could last days or weeks. That meant I had to steal more to get through the dry times.

"But I learned a lot and knew I needed to make some changes. I had to work smarter and expand my criminal activities to earn more. Instead of shaking down the dealers for money, I started shaking them down for product and set up my own network of dealers. And instead of just stealing parts off a car, I took the whole thing. I wanted to get into the chop-shop business and start making some real money."

3

Making Connections

Andrew was ambitious and made a commitment to advance his criminal career. He dropped out of school to allow himself more time on the streets. However, before he fully implemented his bold plans, an event took place that had unintended consequences. Although it resulted in his first arrest, it also brought him to the attention of Gambino crew boss Nicky Corozzo and catapulted him from an unaffiliated street tough into the world of organized crime.

In November 1982, Andrew and a friend learned that a couple of neighborhood boys working in a bagel shop at East 81st Street and Flatlands Avenue were stealing up to $1,500 a week from the place. Andrew and his pal saw this as an opportunity to make some easy cash.

"The owners weren't around that much, especially at night. The night-shift workers made the bagels, served customers, and handled the cash register, pocketing a lot of the money for themselves. Both were in their late teens. The word was that they had serious gambling problems and needed the money to pay off their gambling debts.

"My buddy Tommy and I figured we might as well cut ourselves in on the action. We told them we wanted four or five hundred a week or else. They said okay and didn't resist at all. They started making their payments right away with no problem.

"But the first sign of trouble came quick. This neighborhood guy named Mike Yannotti had a talk with Tommy and me. Mike, who was known on the streets as Mikey Y, was a couple years older than us and was already connected with Nicky Corozzo's crew. He had a reputation as a tough guy and he was. In fact, I met a lot of dangerous guys over the years and in my opinion, Mikey Y was the most dangerous of them all.

"Mike told us that the bagel-shop guys we were shaking down owed Nicky Corozzo a lot of money from gambling. If we continued making them pay us, they couldn't pay him too. We better back off.

"After that conversation, Tommy and I had to make a decision. We were a little pissed off that we were told to stop the shakedown without being offered some other way to replace that income. We said to hell with Nicky Corozzo; we weren't backing down."

That decision would probably have led to another less friendly visit from Mike Yannotti. But something else happened first.

A couple of weeks later, one of the teens got caught by the owners of the bagel shop with his hand in the register. He told his boss that Tommy and Andrew had forced him into stealing the money and giving it to them. The owners called the cops, then headed across the street to the park where Tommy and Andrew hung out to confront them.

"At that time we carried brass knuckles. When the brothers grabbed us, the knuckles came out and the fight was on. We beat one of them up pretty good. I think he ended up needing about a hundred stitches in his head. During the heat of things, a cop grabbed me from behind and spun me around. Tommy and I threw the brass knuckles, but the cops found one set of them. We were arrested, taken to the station, and charged with assault. We were never charged or even questioned about the extortion scheme."

Andrew hired a lawyer who argued that the owners initiated the fight. In fact, Andrew and Tommy pressed assault charges against them and the whole thing ended up in a draw. All charges were dropped and everyone walked away clean.

After that, Andrew started spending more time with Mikey Y and some other guys in Corozzo's crew. Even though he wasn't part of them yet, they did a lot of stealing and some other things. They all made money, some of which went to Nicky.

A couple of months later in early 1983, Andrew met Nicky in person. At that time Nicky hadn't been made an official capo yet. He was an acting capo. Nicky and his friend Leonard DiMaria ran the crew together as co-captains. Andrew already knew Lenny. He'd taken his daughter to the high-school prom and hung around with his nephew. But he'd never met Nicky before.

"They used to hold meetings at a private social club every Tuesday and Saturday. The meetings started around eleven in the morning and went until four or five in the afternoon. The crew members and others they did business with attended.

"One Saturday morning, I was riding in a car with some of the crew. I knew they had to go to the meeting, so I told them to drop me off and I'd see 'em later. One of the guys said that Nicky mentioned they should bring me along. So I went.

"When we got to the club, I was introduced around. Everybody socialized while Nicky conducted business in another room. He called in his people one at a time. In private he told them what he wanted done; they let him know if they needed something from him. If he had a job that involved more than one guy or the entire crew, he called them all in at once.

"Nicky approached me around mid-afternoon and took me into the other room. He said he'd heard a lot about me and knew I was acquainted with his nephews. I was doing some good things. 'You've got a friend here,' he said.

"Then he told me that if I ever needed anything to come to him. If I needed stolen merchandise disposed of, come to him. If somebody was giving me trouble, come to him. Whatever I needed, come to him.

"After that he told me about the Tuesday and Saturday meetings. I'll never forget what he said. 'These meetings are important. You'll meet a lot of people and make a lot of friends. Some of them may need your help sometime. Think of it as going to school. You'll learn valuable lessons here, so don't miss. If you miss, you're not being a good friend.'

"When I left the social club that day, I was officially part of Nicky's crew. I was an associate of the Gambino organized-crime family."

NICKY AND LENNY

Who were these men whom Andrew describes as co-captains of his Gambino family crew? The following is a brief look at their backgrounds and status around the time Andrew became affiliated with them.

Nicholas "Nicky" Corozzo was born in Brooklyn, New York, on March 17, 1940. His brother Joseph "Jo Jo" Corozzo joined Nick in his affiliation with the Gambino family and rose to be the criminal organization's consigliere. Nicky's son-in-law, Vincent Dragonetti, also reputedly became a Gambino associate. And his nephew, Joseph Corozzo Jr., later became involved with the family as a high-profile defense attorney. In the early 1980s, Nick was a chief rival to John Gotti and the two men despised each other. The politics of the situation prevented Nick's official advancement to capo.

Lenny DiMaria was a year younger than Nicky. The close

friends shared the leadership of a Gambino street crew as unofficial capos. In 1981 Lenny was arrested on federal charges of possession of contraband cigarettes. Convicted at trial, he was sentenced to serve 10 years in a federal prison. However, he remained free pending an appeal.

The case was argued in the Second Circuit on November 23, 1983, and decided on February 6, 1984. The conviction was affirmed and Lenny had to surrender and begin serving his sentence. Thus, for most of Andrew's time with the crew, he was under the control of Nicky Corozzo.

Andrew believes Lenny's forced absence from the crew had an adverse affect on his life.

"Lenny was approachable. He was down to earth. You could talk to him about personal things, like if you were having trouble at home. But Nicky wasn't like that. He was in gangster mode all the time. Everything had to be done according to protocol. You had to be very careful of what you said to him. He sometimes took things you told him as signs of weakness. And Nicky didn't want any weak members in his crew.

"Lenny was popular with guys from other crews, but a lot of them didn't like Nicky. Even while he was in prison, guys asked me what we heard from Lenny and how he was doing. They only asked about Nicky as an afterthought. Lenny was much more personable, no doubt about it."

4

Up and Coming

After becoming a member of Nick Corozzo's crew, Andrew refocused on enhancing his budding criminal career.

He knew that stealing cars to sell whole or as parts could be a lucrative business. He also knew that in order to get started, the thieves needed enough space to operate and the skill to dismantle multiple brands of vehicles. Equally important, they had to know what vehicles and parts were in demand and how much money they would bring. And it was critical to have a client base to assure the rapid turnover of inventory.

Andrew decided to take advantage of his newfound connections to get his education in the car-stealing business from an accomplished professional.

"I figured I might as well learn from the best, so I hooked up with an older guy named Anthony Gerbino. Anthony's street name was Beansy and he was affiliated with the Gambino's Roy DeMeo crew. At the time they ran the biggest stolen car ring in the country. Anthony and I quickly developed a teacher-and-student relationship and became fast friends in spite of the age difference."

It was the right choice for Andrew. He learned quickly and by mid-1983, the 17-year-old had become one of the premier car thieves in New York City.

THE CAR BUSINESSES

In the parlance of Andrew DiDonato and Anthony Gerbino, "drop-off" meant the delivery of a vehicle that had been ordered by a customer. Automobile junk yards and body shops were on their list of clients, as well as other thieves and private individuals.

"We stole almost every night, doing drop-offs for neighborhood car shops and junk yards. We filled orders for DeMeo crew members too. One of them was Patty Testa, who was an auto-crime legend."

Testa ran a used-car dealership, Patty Testa's Motor Car Service, and several of the vehicles they stole for him ended up on his lot with altered Vehicle Identification Numbers. Testa made a lot of money in the car business, both legal and illegal.

"But when I got involved with Patty, the DeMeo crew was on its way out. Most of them were already under indictment. Patty himself got convicted on a federal racketeering charge in 1985 and went away for two years. When he got out, he switched to the Lucchese family."

Patty Testa was hit on December 2, 1992, murdered in the garage of his car lot. No one was ever charged for his killing.

● ● ●

Depending on the make and model, Andrew and Anthony made between $300 and $500 per car when they filled orders for their drop-off customers. Their fee was relatively low per unit, but they made up for it in volume.

"The way we worked the deliveries and getting paid was simple. The customers didn't want the hot cars parked right in front of their businesses. We parked the vehicle a little way down the block and left the sun visor down to help the customer identify it. We made three or four deliveries a week to most of these places. They paid us weekly, rather than having to make personal contact on each delivery.

"We had higher paying customers too. Two brothers on Staten Island, who lived a few doors away from Gambino boss Paul Castellano, dealt in exotic brands like Porsche and Ferrari. They paid us three grand per unit. It was a good relationship and we delivered a lot of cars to them. And it was an all-cash business, of course."

In addition to the drop-offs, Andrew and Anthony also stripped or chopped cars.

"Stripping a car meant we took most of the parts, but the car could still be driven. We usually took the wheels and tires and replaced them with what we called baloney [used] tires, so we could move the car around. Chopping a car meant we took everything; there was nothing left. We used to joke that we turned a chopped car into a Pepsi can."

Like good entrepreneurs, Andrew and Anthony invested some of their earnings to expand their business.

"We rented garages to dismantle cars and store inventory. For the parts business, we bought work trucks to make deliveries. Overall, General Motors makes—Olds, Caddy, Pontiac, and Chevy—were the most popular. And as the business grew, we brought in more people to help dispose of inventory. We had a scrap-metal guy, an engine guy, a glass specialist, and a tire and wheel man. We profited from every part of the car. Nothing went to waste.

"And we had to have more thieves to help keep up with the orders. Mike Yannotti worked with us regularly. Another neighborhood guy named Albert Lattanzi stole with us."

Although there was good money in stolen cars and parts, another aspect of the business was even more profitable. Andrew refers to it as "the rebuildables."

"In the rebuildables business, we legally bought wrecked or recovered stolen vehicles dirt cheap. Then we went out the same night, stole the exact same car as we'd bought, and rebuilt the one we owned legally. Within a few weeks, we sold it at full book value. There was a small fortune to be made and we made it."

THE SHELL CHASE

One incident from those days stands out for Andrew.

One of his friends had an old Mercedes he was rebuilding and asked Andrew to steal a duplicate to strip for the parts. Anthony, Albert, and Andrew found the exact car, stole it, and brought it to Sally the Lip's house on East 86th Street. By the time they were finished with it, all that was left was the frame and engine—no glass, mirrors, hood, trunk lid, or seats, not even the Nardi steering wheel. They put on a set of baloney tires so Andrew could drive the shell a few blocks away and leave it on the street.

That night they crimped all the oil lines so no trail led back to the garage. Sally went to the corner and used a flashlight to signal the coast was clear. Sitting on an overturned milk crate and using Vise-Grip pliers to steer, Andrew drove the shell out of the garage, Albert following behind in the work car.

"A kid with a Lucchese crew that lived in the neighborhood was also in the car business and the Auto Squad knew it. The cops were watching his house that night. When I passed by, they got a look at what I was driving. I saw their lights come on and knew I had to make a run for it.

"That Mercedes could fly with nothing on it and I was doing over a hundred real quick. I had no way to see where the cop car was, but I could hear the siren right behind me. I ran a couple of red lights and was coming up on Ralph Avenue, a major intersection. I decided to take a chance and run that red light too and see if the cops had balls enough to follow me. I said a little prayer and hit the intersection doing over a hundred. I just missed getting T-boned and made it through.

Behind me I heard the screeching of brakes and knew the cop had run out of nerve.

"I kept going a few more blocks and made a left on East Fifty-eighth. By this time the oil lines had exploded and the car was enveloped in a big cloud of smoke. I pulled over and left the car at the intersection of Avenue K and took off running. I saw a cop car coming toward me and ducked behind a telephone pole while they passed. When they got to East Fifty-eighth, they must have seen the cloud of smoke, because they turned and headed in that direction.

"Just then Albert Lattanzi showed up in the work car. I ran across the street and jumped in. I think the cops who had just gone by might have caught sight of me running, but it was too late for them to do anything. We were already gone.

"After we got a few blocks away, Albert reached over and felt my chest to see how fast my heart was beating. He said the whole scene was like something out of a movie. I guess maybe it was."

EXTORTION

In addition to the stolen-car operation, Andrew's involvement in the drug trade had increased dramatically in scope and profitability. From initially shaking down a handful of young marijuana dealers by himself, Andrew and his gang were now muscling older dealers selling heavier drugs, such as cocaine. These were large-scale operators whose suppliers protected them. This made the situation a lot more dangerous than it was with the pot dealers.

"We went to a known drug-dealer spot. We grabbed the dealer at gunpoint, forced him to a pay phone, and made him call his supplier for a delivery [later on, beepers replaced pay phones]. When the runner showed up, we robbed him of his money and product. After that, we made him tell us everything we needed to know about their operation, like who was involved, where they operated, and where they kept their inventory.

"And then we went there. We usually put a gun to the guy's head and said, 'Listen, either you're going to pay us a thousand a week or we're gonna kill you right here, right now.' A few guys challenged us and had to be forced into line. But most of them agreed to pay without a fight.

"After we got a few guys like that under our belt, we started going to every major drug dealer we could find. In a fairly short time, we had most of the major dealers in the Canarsie, Mill Basin, and Flatbush sections of Brooklyn paying us.

"We didn't get 'em all, though. Two guys operating out of the housing projects were strong [they had a large organization] and well-insulated. And they were no strangers to violence. If we caught up with them, there was a good chance we'd have had to kill one of them to get the point across.

"They knew we were after them. We were never able to get the information we needed to catch them. Every time we got close, we ran into some kind of obstacle. Eventually, we just walked away and went after other guys."

ROAD RAGE SHOOTING

For Andrew, 1983 was a big year. He joined Corozzo's crew and fine-tuned his abilities as a thief and extortionist. He began carrying a gun on a regular basis. But something else happened that year that made him even more valuable to Nicky. He proved he was capable of violence beyond using his fists or a baseball bat.

"My first shooting incident happened early one morning right around dawn. Jo Jo [Nicky's nephew Joseph Corozzo, Jr.] and I had been out all night. We were on our way home and Jo Jo was driving his father's Mercedes. I was in the passenger seat and starting to nod off. A friend of ours in another car and Jo Jo started playing a game of chicken.

"But some other guy was on the road with his girlfriend. This guy got pissed off and him and Jo Jo exchanged words and obscene gestures. When we stopped at a light, this guy pulled up behind us. In the rearview mirror, Jo Jo saw him get out of his car and start running up the passenger side of our car. Jo Jo hollered to me in an excited voice, 'Wake up, Andrew! Wake up! Shoot him, Andrew! Shoot him!'

"I looked in the side mirror and saw this guy coming up toward my door. He was carrying a big knife, like a Bowie knife. I lowered the window and pulled my gun. When he grabbed my door handle, I swung around and shot him in the groin area. He dropped to the pavement and Jo Jo took off. We ran a red light and I saw some people at a bus stop as we rounded the corner. I fired a few shots in the air to scare them away, so they wouldn't pay much attention to us or the car. We got away with no problem.

"I reported what happened to Nicky right away and he called me down to the club. He wasn't happy. He said his brother [Jo Jo, Sr.] was pretty upset. He was hiding out in Florida at the time, ducking a subpoena, and didn't need his car involved at the scene of a shooting. I explained to Nicky that this guy was coming at me with a knife and I didn't have many options. He said okay, it would be taken care of. But he added that I might have to make it up to his brother by going to Florida and doing some work for him.

"Jo Jo Senior wanted to get the shooting mess cleaned up. He found out which hospital the guy I shot was in and sent two of his men to see him. They told him they knew his wound wasn't life threatening. They had ten thousand dollars in cash with them and were prepared to give it to him right then and that would be the end of it. If he didn't take the money and wanted to cooperate with the police investigation instead, his wound would become fatal and he wouldn't leave the hospital alive. He took the money and that's the last I heard about it."

● ● ●

As 1983 ended Andrew was becoming a very active and valuable member of the Corozzo crew. He was loyal, an accomplished thief, and a good producer. He'd also developed a reputation as a tough kid who was willing to use a gun. These were all qualities men like Nicky Corozzo looked for in their subordinates.

Over the next several years, Andrew continued to hone his criminal skills and was given more responsibilities by his boss.

5

1984

Andrew's mother Patrina was no stranger to having criminals in the family. Her husband Vincent was in federal prison from 1966, the year following Andrew's birth, to 1971 after being convicted of hijacking a truck and criminal possession of a weapon. And, of course, Vincent's uncle Paddy Macchiarole had been a Genovese family capo.

Patrina and Vincent never got back together after he was released from prison. She remarried in 1975. In 1984, the family, consisting of Patrina, her husband Morris, Andrew, and his twin sisters, lived near the intersection of East 72nd Street and Bergen Court in Brooklyn.

"My mother knew what I was doing and she didn't approve. But I was on the cusp of becoming a man and my course was laid out. There was nothing she could do about it. She had no choice but to accept what I was. She was my confidant, very protective and always worried about my safety.

"My sisters were three years older than me. They knew how I made my money too. I'm not saying they were happy, but they never hassled me about it. One of them got married and moved out in 1983. The other one got married the following year.

"My father remained in Brooklyn after serving his sentence. We saw each other from time to time. We never had a normal father-and-son relationship. It was more of a big-brother type. He was a career gambler with a gift of gab who was in and out of my life.

"As a boy and young man I craved my father's attention and acceptance. As I got deeper into the life with each passing year, I hoped he'd look upon me with the same respect I'd seen him show for Paddy. I never saw my father talk so highly of anyone as he did his uncle.

"With that idea in my head, I tried to follow Paddy's footsteps into the world of organized crime. I carried myself in the same manner and my reputation grew. But my father was still years away from seeing me the way I wanted him to."

Although Andrew's relationship with his father in 1984 wasn't exactly the way he hoped it would be, his association with the Corozzo faction of the Gambino family became rock solid.

TROUBLE WITH THE LUCCHESES—PART I

For Andrew, the year 1984 literally began with a bang as he tended to some unfinished business from 1983. The matter involved an ongoing feud with a crew from another organized-crime group, the Lucchese family. This particular Lucchese crew operated in the same areas as Nick Corozzo's. It was run by Anthony "Gaspipe" Casso and his friend Vittorio "Vic" Amuso. Both men were known killers and extremely dangerous to have as enemies.

The trouble began in 1983 when Vic Amuso's nephew had an altercation with Andrew's friend and fellow Corozzo crew member, Sal "Sally the Lip" Bracchi.

"Vic's nephew and some of his friends from Gaspipe's crew tuned Sally the Lip up [beat him] pretty good. We wanted to retaliate and send a message that you didn't fuck around with our guys. The kid knew we were after him and kept a low profile. It took a long time, but in early 1984 we found out that he was gonna be spending the night at a home right around the corner from the sixty-ninth police precinct on Foster Avenue in Canarsie.

"That night me, Anthony Gerbino, and Albert Lattanzi went to that house and broke into the garage, opening the overhead door just enough to crawl under. There were two cars inside. We'd brought gasoline with us and doused both cars. As we left, we let the gas run down the driveway and make a stream leading to the vehicles. Once we were safely outside, we lit a rag, threw it into the little river of gasoline, and got out of there.

"Somehow the garage door closed when we left, so all the gas fumes were confined inside. When the flame reached the cars, there was a tremendous explosion. The garage door was blown all the way across the street. The heat was so intense that every one of the tires blew out. Nobody in the house got hurt; it was property damage only. But we'd sent a message and figured it was just a matter of time before Gaspipe's boys figured out who had delivered it."

EASTER BREAK

After putting the Lucchese crew on notice, Andrew had another obligation to take care of: working off his debt to Jo Jo Corozzo in Florida for the 1983 road-rage shooting incident. That trip took place in mid-April and lasted for three weeks or so.

"Me and several of the crew flew down," Andrew recalls. "There was Mike Yannotti, Albert Lattanzi, and four or five other guys. Jo Jo treated all of us great. If he was pissed off at me, he didn't show it.

"We had a lot of fun and did a lot of partying. But we worked too. We did some major credit-card fraud and made some big money."

The fraud involved buying stolen credit cards, then making purchases or taking cash advances on them. In addition to the profits, the scam carried an element of risk and excitement.

"We bought the hot cards for three hundred apiece. Back in New York, guys we knew who had credit card machines swiped the cards and told us how much credit was available. We didn't have those connections in Florida, so we operated blind. When we presented these cards to a merchant or a bank, we never knew for sure what was going to happen.

"We used them to cover our hotel rooms. Sometimes we'd come back to the hotel and be locked out after the card went over the limit. When that happened, we just tried a different card. Other times we found out the cops were looking for us, because when the hotel ran the card, it came back as stolen. In those cases, we had to clear out and find a different hotel.

"The same thing could happen when we bought stuff at a store. The merchant might tell us the sale exceeded the credit limit. If the card had already been reported as stolen, we could usually tell by the clerk's expression and body language. Once in a while one of them tried to get us to hang around until they could get the cops there. They said something like, 'Excuse me for a minute while I go in the back room and check on something. I'll be right back, so don't leave.' That was pretty transparent and we were long gone before the door to the back room even had a chance to close.

"And not all the store clerks were honest either. I remember one decided to do some stealing for himself. He told us the card was bad after we tried to charge twelve hundred dollars worth of clothing. But I'd seen him write the authorization number down on a sheet of paper, so he could use it after we left. I jumped across the counter and wrapped the phone cord around his throat, while my partner in crime gave him a beating. He confessed what he was up to. After that we owned him and he worked for us from that point on running the hot cards."

Andrew and his friends finished their stay in Florida and made it back to New York without incident. But the bad blood between them and Gaspipe's crew hadn't cooled during their absence. If anything, it had heated up.

TROUBLE WITH THE LUCCHESES—PART II

When Andrew left New York to visit Jo Jo Corozzo, Sr., in Florida, the feud with the Lucchese crew was in the Gaspipe gang's court. The next move was theirs. Shortly after his return to the Big Apple, he got their response.

"On a Friday night, I was at a bar we ran on Avenue L in Canarsie. Somebody told me Nicky was outside in his car and wanted to see me. I went out and found Nicky and his driver sitting in their car. I was standing beside the passenger door with my head inside the window talking. Rocco Corozzo, Nicky's nephew, came outside and joined us. We were engaged in conversation when out of the corner of my eye, I noticed a figure standing on the sidewalk fifty or so yards away. Then I heard what I thought were firecrackers, but they turned out to be gunshots.

"One round struck the windshield right in front of where Nicky was sitting. I shoved his head down and Rocco jumped in the back seat. After Nicky's car sped away, I pulled my gun [a 9mm] and started running toward the shooter, firing at him as I ran. He took off down the block and at that point, I went down on one knee and aimed. I call that my T. J. Hooker position, after the old television series where William Shatner played a cop. I fired and missed. I reloaded and started chasing the guy, but I couldn't catch him.

"A few days later we got information on who the shooter was and why. It was one of Gaspipe's guys. I was the target in retaliation for the incident at the house where Vic Amuso's nephew had been staying.

"I took the information to Nicky. I told him we wanted to pursue it and asked what he wanted us to do. Nicky was a very cunning man. He'd never come right out and tell you to murder somebody. But he made the sign of a gun with his index finger and thumb. He said to me, 'Go and teach this guy a lesson.'

"That night we went out and stole two cars and stashed them. One would be used in the attack when we found this kid and his buddies. The other would be left where we could get to it for use as a getaway car after the shooting. After a while we learned they hung out at a bar on Flatlands Avenue in Canarsie. Across the street from the bar was a funeral parlor. Albert Lattanzi, Anthony Gerbino, a kid named Richie, and me drove one of the stolen cars to the funeral parlor and parked in the lot. A U-Haul truck was already parked there. It turns out the guys we were looking for left the bar and all of them loaded into that U-Haul truck. The shooter who had tried to kill me was identified as being in the group. That was it. The target was acquired and we were going after them.

"We followed them until they rolled up to a stop sign. We pulled alongside the truck. Anthony was driving and Richie was in the front seat with him. Albert was in the back seat driver side and I was on the passenger side.

"Richie opened fire first with a shotgun. He shot out the front tire and the engine. The truck was stopped dead in its tracks. I fired next, throwing a couple of rounds into the back of the truck. I was far enough back that I couldn't get a good shot at the guys in the cab. I leaned out the window as far as I could and let a couple of rounds go at them anyway. After I emptied my clip, Albert sat on the driver-side rear window sill and fired at the truck across the roof of our car. We then drove away to where we had left the getaway car.

"During the drive, Richie went into a panic. He started whining, saying things like, 'Andrew, what did you do? We're gonna go away for murder.'

"I told him, 'What the fuck did you think we came here for tonight? You threw the first shot.' After a while he calmed down.

"We made it to the second car and drove that back to our hangout. Mike Yannotti was waiting there and we told him what went down. He then torched both of the cars we'd used to destroy any evidence.

"At that time I assumed we'd killed one or more people. And then we got word that nobody was dead. Our main target was injured, but he'd survive. It was disappointing at the time. But looking back at it now, I thank God it turned out that way."

● ● ●

Following that incident, Gaspipe Casso made his displeasure with Andrew known to Nicky Corozzo. He wanted Andrew dead and expected Nicky to agree that his young crewman deserved to be executed. When the two bosses got together to discuss the matter, Nicky played his trump card.

"Mob protocol says that you can't kill a made man without getting permission for the hit," Andrew explains. "Up until that meeting, Gaspipe wasn't aware that Nicky had been sitting in the car that night and a bullet had struck the windshield right in front of him. When Gaspipe said he wanted me for the torch job on the house Amuso's nephew was at and the U-Haul thing, Nicky said, 'You want this kid for that? Let me tell you something. I was sitting in the goddamn car the night your guy started shooting. One of the bullets hit the windshield right in front of my fuckin' head. I was lucky not to be killed. What about that?'

"That was the end of the conversation. Nicky had made his point. And under the circumstances, Gaspipe had nowhere else to go with his beef. That should have been the end of it. With a guy like Gaspipe, though, you always had to wonder if it would be."

Gaspipe Casso didn't get Andrew. But the law eventually got Gaspipe and Vic Amuso. Both are currently in federal prison serving sentences of life without parole for racketeering.

THE MURDER OF ALBERT LATTANZI

That same year, Andrew suffered the loss of two people he was very close to in a two-month period. The first came in June when his paternal grandmother Amelia Macchiarole DiDonato passed away. Her death hit Andrew particularly hard.

"My sisters, my mother, and I lived with her while my father was incarcerated. She was the best there was. She took care of all the kids. She had seventeen grandchildren, but we were the only three grandkids that lived with her. She was the glue that held the family together. There were always a lot of people at her house and she fed everybody. She was very generous. When she died, it affected everybody."

Andrew was still grieving over the loss of his grandmother when the second shoe dropped in August. This time it wasn't a blood relative, but the death was equally devastating. His close personal friend and crewmate Albert Lattanzi, one of the neighborhood guys Andrew first stole cars with, was murdered.

"Because of the trouble we'd had with Gaspipe's guys, Nicky told us to lay low until he could make sure everything was taken care of. He wanted to calm us down, so to speak. Mike Yannotti, Anthony Gerbino, Richie, Albert, and me were moving around a lot, staying in various places and with different friends around Brooklyn.

"One night Albert said he wanted to go out. I told him to hang around the house we were at. I said we were going to order some Chinese food and rent a couple of movies. He said the rest of us were having girlfriends over and he just needed to get out. He planned to go out on Long Island where he wasn't likely to run into anybody that knew him. I couldn't force him to stay at the apartment, so he went. He usually carried a gun, but on that night he went unarmed."

Albert hooked up with a guy from their crew named Mario and a Lucchese associate named Bobby. Bobby wasn't with the Gaspipe crew and he was friendly with Andrew's crew. But instead of going to Long Island, they went to a new dance club on Coney Island Avenue in Brooklyn.

At the club, Albert met up with a girl; she was Mike Yannotti's cousin. They talked for a while and she said she needed a ride home when the club closed. Albert told her he'd make sure she got home okay. She then left Albert to socialize.

Later on, she started dancing with a guy named Evan, a drug dealer for the Lucchese family. They'd muscle him into working for them the same way Andrew did with dealers in his neighborhood. She and Evan hit it off.

When it was time to go, Albert and Evan got into an argument over who'd drive the girl home. That deteriorated into a fistfight. As they rolled around on the ground, Todd Alvino, one of the Lucchese guys Evan was dealing for, walked up, drew his gun, and shot Albert dead. Alvino had a bad cocaine problem and it's likely he was hopped up at the time.

Andrew picks up the story. "After Alvino shot Albert, he turned the gun on Mario. The gun either jammed or was out of rounds and didn't fire. Mario was a legitimate tough guy and he was armed. For some reason he froze. He never pulled his gun to avenge Albert or defend himself. He was damn lucky to get out of the place alive. Alvino commandeered a car and got away.

"When we got the call that Albert had been murdered, we wanted Alvino bad. Mike, Anthony, Richie, and me geared up [armed themselves]. We stole a car from a neighbor and headed out looking for revenge. We knew Alvino's father ran a newsstand in the neighborhood and that he'd be there in the morning to open up. We decided to kill him for starters. But as we calmed down and began thinking more clearly, we discarded that idea. We all had fathers. They were civilians and Alvino's old man didn't have anything to do with Albert's death. We went out looking for his son, though, but couldn't find him. Alvino surrendered to the cops a few days later, then got out on bail.

"From that point forward, the hunt was on. We literally worked in shifts and stalked him night and day. We went to known Lucchese hangouts, bars, social clubs, and after-hours joints. We kept an eye on his house on Ralph Avenue. We came close a couple of times, but couldn't catch up with him.

"Alvino and the Luccheses knew we were looking for him, of course. Nicky was onboard with what we were doing, but in order to prevent the Lucchese bosses from requesting a sit-down that would have stopped the hunt, Nicky had to deny that Albert had been part of his crew. That way he could say the whole thing was none of his business.

"Even though we were after Alvino around the clock, he dodged us month after month. Nicky mentioned the amount of time it was taking. He said, 'If this happened to a friend of Lenny and me, the guy that did it would be dead already.'

"Another time I was talking with Nicky in a small social club we hung out at on East Ninety-Third Street at Avenue L in Canarsie. The Luccheses had a club in the back of a laundromat right across the street. Nicky pointed to a car parked out in front and said, 'What if I told you I know that by the end of the day, the guy you're looking for is going to get into that car?'

"I said that I'd stay right there and shoot him when he showed up. Nicky said, 'No you won't. But I'll tell you what you will do. You'll take him down the block and shoot him. But you won't shoot him in front of our club.' I waited around, but Alvino never came."

In spite of the best efforts of Andrew and his friends, the elusive Todd Alvino remained alive.

OOPS

In the world of organized crime, problems can arise from inside the family as well as from outside. Later in the year, Andrew made an honest mistake that could have had serious consequences.

One Friday night, Nicky called a meeting at the Seaview Diner on Rockaway Parkway in Canarsie. Anthony Gerbino, Mike Yannotti, Richie, and Andrew drove out there in their work car, which was registered and insured in the name of a dead woman. When they pulled into the parking lot, they noticed a guy talking on the pay phone on the street and a Mercedes convertible at the curb next to him, engine running.

They went inside the restaurant. Nicky wasn't there yet, so they hung around, talking with some of the other guys. Pretty soon, a made man with the Gambinos they knew came in and asked if they were still in the car business. He mentioned the Mercedes and figured they'd be interested in it.

"The four of us went back outside. Mike would grab the car. I'd get between the car and the guy on the phone. Richie and Anthony went to the work car. As soon as Mike got away, I'd hop in with them and we'd follow Mike back to my place.

"Mike had just gotten in the car when 'Pay Phone' spotted him. He made a dash for the car and I gave him a hip check that sent him rolling into the street. He got up and made a grab for the passenger-door handle, but Mike pulled away before he could reach it. I got in the work car and we took off.

"We got to my house and barely got inside when the phone rang. It was Nicky. He said, 'Have you guys still got that thing you took from the diner?' I told him yeah, we've got it. He said, 'We've got a little problem. Just stay there and don't do anything. I'll get back to you in a few minutes.'

"As soon as I hung up the phone, we went through the car. We found a wallet in the glove compartment and a satchel in the trunk and took them inside. Inside the satchel were a bunch of white envelopes and a ledger book with a thirty-eight revolver on top of them. I opened the first envelope and there was fifteen hundred in cash in it. We opened the rest and the total came to eighty-seven thousand dollars. It was obvious that the Mercedes didn't belong to some ordinary citizen. There was a clue on the envelopes; the logo on them said Meats Supreme. That was one of Paul Castellano's legitimate businesses. But in our excitement over all that money, we didn't pay any attention.

"About then Nicky called back. He said, 'There's a bag in the trunk of that car. Whatever you do, don't open that bag.' I hung up the phone and when we got done laughing, Nicky called for the third time. He said, 'I found out there's a book in that bag too. That book's gotta be kept safe, understand? Don't look in it and don't let anything happen to it.'

"You know what we did next, right? The book was full of names and dollar amounts and phone numbers. It was becoming clear that we'd taken a car used to collect payoffs and had something to do with Paul Castellano. But what?

"We checked the license plate and looked through the wallet from the glove compartment. The Mercedes belonged to a relative of Paul's and no doubt some or all of the money was intended for Paul. As much as it hurt, there was no doubt we'd have to give back the car and the cash. The question was would the Castellanos let it go at that or would they want to teach us a lesson.

"We met up with Nicky late that night at Sally the Lip's house. Nicky told us, 'I'd never ask you to give back something you stole. But this is the one time I'm going to. Everything's gotta be returned.' He said he'd set up a meet for the next morning at a luncheonette at East Ninety-Third Street and Avenue L across from our social club.

"We didn't know how pissed the Castellanos were and we weren't about to take any chances. We went to the meet armed to the teeth in case we had to shoot our way out. Mike Yannotti and I went first with the money, the book, and the wallet. We emptied the bullets out of the gun and took that too. Anthony Gerbino brought the Mercedes over a few minutes later.

"Nicky was there and so was Paul's relative Pay Phone. He had a couple of guys with him, but they were okay. Pay Phone hugged Nicky and thanked him and us for doing the right thing. There was even one thing that got a chuckle from everybody. That was when we told Pay Phone the cash was ten dollars short. He was running the Mercedes on empty when we took it and we had to put gas in it to get it back to him. We figured that was his expense and not ours.

"Mike, Anthony, and I were a little pissed that all we got was a thank you. The next day we had our Saturday meeting at the club. Nicky said he'd gotten a phone call. Paul Castellano told him we'd earned a feather in our cap for doing the honorable thing, and we had personal favors coming if we ever needed them.

"I said to Nicky as a joke, 'Favors don't pay the bills. Maybe he can give us that eighty-seven thousand back.' A couple of days later a fruit basket was delivered to my house. The card said, 'You did a very honorable thing. Your friend Paul.'

"Although I would have preferred the money, there were a few times over the next several months that having that connection with Castellano came in handy."

BUSINESS SUFFERS

As the year passed, the intense focus by Andrew and his crewmates to find and kill Todd Alvino eventually hurt them in the wallet.

"When you're not out there stealing, you're not earning,"

Andrew explained. "We were spending more time looking for Alvino than we were working. It came to a point that the lack of income was noticeable."

In order to compensate, they changed how they shook down the pot dealers. Rather than handing over $500 a week, the dealers now gave them two pounds of marijuana. A friend of Andrew's stood in Utica Park at Utica Avenue and Avenue N, selling dime bags of marijuana. Pretty soon he was making $500-$600 a day. His cut was three bags out of every 20 he sold, $30 out of the $200. Andrew also got permission to have another friend deal in the Bensonhurst section of Brooklyn.

"I was making four or five thousand a week. But I shared that with Mike, Anthony, and Richie, and I had to send Nicky an envelope every week. The four of us ended up with about eight hundred a week each. But we were still extorting money from some of the big drug dealers. We kept that as kind of a slush fund, in case we needed bail money or something. Nicky got a piece of that too, only it was on a monthly basis."

As 1984 drew to a close, Andrew, not yet 20 years old, was keeping his head above water financially. But the frustration over not being able to locate Todd Alvino was growing by the day.

6

1985

As a rule, criminals aren't overly fond of being stopped and questioned by the police, especially if they happen to be in possession of items that are illegal or difficult to explain away. Andrew was confronted with that exact situation in January.

Anthony Gerbino, Mike Yannotti, and Andrew were driving to a friend's nightclub in Mike's 1983 Fleetwood when a squad car pulled them over. Andrew was carrying two illegal guns and Mike had one. It was Super Bowl weekend and Andrew was also carrying about twenty thousand dollars in bets. As the officer was approaching the car, they decided they couldn't afford a search. Mike handed him the registration and insurance card, then sped off. The chase was on. They had enough of a head start that they were able to ditch the guns. Andrew hid the money.

By that time, several more police cars had joined the pursuit and it turned into a regular demolition derby, the Cadillac against New York's finest. They ran a couple of cruisers off the road and smashed fenders with another one. When they got behind a car stopped at a red light, they went right through, pushing it in front of them. It ended when a police car T-boned the caddy on Flatbush Avenue.

Fifteen or so very pissed off officers took turns beating

up the three occupants. If a few citizens hadn't stopped to see what was going on, it could have been more serious, maybe even deadly. All three ended up bruised and needing stitches.

The charges included possession of weapons, for a blackjack and ball bats in the trunk. The police also found the money Andrew had hidden. They couldn't charge him with anything for that, but they did report it to the Organized Crime Task Force to put them all on their radar.

"When we went for arraignment the next morning," Andrew explained, "the judge knew the cops had beaten us during the arrest. We refused to press charges against them, though. The judge made us a deal: If we pled guilty, we'd only have to pay a fine and not do any time. We took it.

"Afterward, we saw some of those same police officers from time to time and there was a mutual respect. That's the way it was back then."

VENGEANCE

On a Friday night in late February, Andrew got the news that after six months of pursuit, Todd Alvino was dead. The murderer of Albert Lattanzi was shot to death outside a dance club on Rockaway Parkway and Avenue N in Canarsie. In a bit of irony, this was the same location that had once been home to the Bamboo Lounge, a known hangout for Lucchese family members and associates. It was torched by Lucchese soldier Henry Hill and that scene was reenacted in the 1990 movie *Goodfellas*.

Andrew was on a date that night, at the Seaview Diner a few blocks from the shooting scene. Someone came in, said a guy was gunned down outside the dance club, and Andrew ran over. The area was roped off and in the middle of it was Alvino's brown Caddy coupe.

Later that night, Andrew learned that Alvino had a passenger with him when he pulled up in front of the club. The passenger went inside to get some cigarettes, while Alvino waited in the car. That's when he was killed.

The next day was the regular Saturday meeting at the social club. Anthony and Mike showed up later than everyone else. As soon as Nicky saw Mike, he moved everybody out of the way and said, "There's my fuckin' man." They shook hands and kissed each other on the cheek. Then Nicky, Mike, and Anthony walked away for a private conversation.

"Nicky treated Mike with a whole different level of respect that day," Andrew remembers. "Like an equal. When I heard about the shooting the previous night, I thought Mike might have been involved in it. But after seeing the way Nicky acted toward him, there was no longer any doubt.

"A couple of days after that, I was talking with Anthony. I told him how happy I was the Alvino thing was over. I just wished I could have been there, because I wanted so bad to avenge Albert. Anthony said, 'It doesn't matter. If you'd have been there, it would have got done. It happened we were there and it got done. The important thing is that it got done.' This was the first actual admission I'd heard that Anthony and Mike had killed Alvino.

"The second came a few weeks later while Mike and I were driving around talking. With Alvino out of the way, we were looking for Evan, the guy who had been fighting with Albert the night Albert was murdered. Mike turned to me, made the sign of a gun with his fingers, and said, 'We put one down. One down and one to go.' We searched for Evan for a while. We found out he'd moved to Florida and eventually lost interest.

"Here's what happened later, though. The cops arrested Albert's stepfather Sal for Todd Alvino's murder. Sal wasn't part of any organized-crime family, but he was a very dangerous man. He was looking for Alvino the same time we were. Sometimes we exchanged information with him about where we thought Todd might be. And sometimes we rode together when we were checking out various locations. So if he was also involved in Todd's killing, it wouldn't surprise me. Anyway, Sal was the only one charged. He was convicted and sent to prison. He died behind bars while serving his sentence.

"The other families and crews had been watching to see how we handled the killing of one of our men. When Albert's murder was finally avenged, it sent the word to them that Nicky Corozzo's crew was a serious operation, one that deserved respect. In that sense, all our crew members were made the day Alvino died."

INDICTMENTS

In March, the imprisoned Lenny DiMaria, along with Nicky Corozzo and John Gotti, were among 10 defendants named in a two-count federal indictment. The first count charged them as leaders of a part of the Gambino crime family, in which they conspired together in the enterprise through "a pattern of racketeering activity" consisting of theft, illegal gambling, extortion, robbery, trafficking in contraband cigarettes, and acts and threats involving murder and robbery. The second count also charged the defendants with racketeering. It alleged 15 racketeering acts, in at least two of which each defendant participated.

WITNESS INTIMIDATION

During the summer, Andrew had to come to the rescue of two of his crewmates, Anthony Gerbino and Mike Yannotti. His assistance was required to discourage a witness, who had seen the pair attempt to steal a car, from cooperating with the police.

"We had a customer order for a red Mercedes convertible. A neighbor of crew-member Vincent Dragonetti had that exact car. We tried to steal it once, but had to abort; the vehicle had a second alarm we weren't prepared for. We left some tools behind, so the owner was aware of the attempt."

One afternoon Anthony and Mike passed that same car parked on the street and tried to steal it again. They popped the hood to see if they could get it started. That drew attention from some of the business owners and pedestrians, so they gave up and left the scene. When the owner arrived and realized there had been another attempt to steal his car, he took action to identify and punish the thieves.

The owner canvassed the area looking for witnesses who could identify the culprits. He found one at the U.S. Military recruiting station. One of the recruiters said he had seen the two guys and would be able to identify them. The owner also filed a complaint with the 69th precinct, which had an Auto Crime Task Force that was already investigating the Gambino and Lucchese car thieves. He even put up reward money for information leading to an arrest.

"All that heat hurt business," Andrew recalls. "And then we heard that there was a witness who was going to finger Anthony and Mike. They found out it was the recruiter and asked me to do whatever it took to get him to keep his mouth shut.

"At this point, my relationship with Mike was strained over some personal issues. You see, Nicky liked his crew to work well together, but not to be too close. Nicky knew that if two guys were fast friends and one of them had to go, the other guy might not be willing to do the work [the killing]. So he became an expert at instigating and causing friction when he sensed crew loyalty might be in question. He put a little wedge between me and Mike, making us more like rivals than friends. That didn't matter, though. There was too much at stake for me to refuse to help. It was also a way for me to extend an olive branch to Mike, so I agreed.

"The next day I walked into the recruiter's office, using the ploy that I was interested in enlisting. After a half-hour conversation, I lured the recruiter outside where my fellow crew member Mario was waiting. We pounced on the guy before he knew what was happening and beat him with our fists and a lead pipe, warning him that if he didn't keep quiet about the car incident, we'd come back and kill him. The recruiter never came forward as a witness and no charges were filed against Anthony or Mike for the attempted theft."

EXPANSION

As 1985 wore on, Andrew became less involved with the car business. He still helped Anthony Gerbino deliver stolen parts, do drop-offs, and move cars around. However, the reduction in the amount of time he devoted to car theft didn't mean he was getting lazy or having second thoughts about being a criminal. Far from it. Andrew was using the extra hours to increase his drug activities and to add a new business to his repertoire: shylocking.

Andrew made friends with some of the guys in the Carmine Persico faction of the Colombo family and they started networking their drug businesses. He became more directly involved in the drug operations and was making lots of money. Then he got permission from Nicky to start putting some serious money out on the street.

"After Nicky was indicted in March, things got pretty tight. Even though he was out on bail, the heat was on and he knew he had to be very cautious about what he did. Business suffered and he expected everybody to keep a lower profile and tighten their belts. He gave me the okay to make the loans, but the money was tightly controlled and only went to low-risk borrowers.

"Here's how shylocking works. Interest is based on the point system. One point equals one dollar of interest on every hundred dollars borrowed. That's a weekly payment, not monthly or annually.

"For example, a six-thousand-dollar loan at three points meant a hundred eighty dollars a week in interest. If I got the money from Nicky at one point, he'd get sixty dollars and I'd get a hundred twenty. I charged different points depending on the size of the loan. More points on small loans because there was less money involved and they got paid off quicker. There were less points on the larger loans, because you didn't want to choke the customer with interest. If I had a real good customer, I'd sometimes give him a deal called a knockdown loan. Under that scenario, for every four weekly payments, two went for interest and two came directly off the principal.

"There was good money in shylocking. But as careful as I was about who I loaned to, every once in a while I'd get a deadbeat I'd have to chase down and get his attention. Overall, though, it was a good business."

SHAKEUP AT THE TOP

On the evening of December 16, Gambino family boss Paul Castellano and his bodyguard and driver Tommy Bilotti were gunned down on the street in front of Sparks Steak House in Manhattan. The killings were carried out on the orders of John Gotti, who had developed a hatred for Castellano. Gotti and his friend and confidant Salvatore "Sammy the Bull" Gravano observed from a car parked across the street as the assassinations were carried out.

Castellano's death elevated Gotti to the throne of power in the family. The new boss' dislike for Nicky Corozzo caused angst in the Corozzo crew. The jailed Lenny DiMaria sent a message from his prison cell: "What's going to be waiting for me when I get out? A bullet?"

● ● ●

For Andrew, the year finished better than it started.

The Todd Alvino matter no longer weighed on him. And the manner in which it was resolved had added to his stature. Although there was uncertainty over the direction the family would take under the leadership of John Gotti, the only problem for Andrew personally was the continuing friction with Mike Yannotti.

7

For Andrew, 1986 could be called the Year of Fraud. It encompassed a fraudulent employment scheme, credit-card fraud, and a scam involving rebuildable cars. It also included a confrontation with a Russian gang over drug turf. However, the year began with romance.

Andrew had dated his share of girls as a teenager and an up-and-coming mobster. Now a streetwise 20-year-old, he entered his first serious relationship. The girl's name was Dina and he was introduced to her by Anthony Gerbino at a club in Sheepshead Bay. Dina was with a guy and they were arguing.

"I walked up to their table and whispered in her ear. I said, 'You can spend the night arguing with him or you can come home with me.' She went home with me. After that night, we were together all the time. I was a year older than her and we were just alike. Too much alike, maybe. Our relationship was passionate and tumultuous."

It began with violence the first day he went to her apartment. Dina told Andrew her ex-boyfriend Ronnie was stalking her. He followed her around and sat outside her window on the fire escape. When Andrew was there, Ronnie started ringing the doorbell. Andrew saw by the look on her face that she was scared. He opened up the door and told Ronnie to beat it. Ronnie wasn't happy with that and they had words.

"I pulled my gun out of my pants and pistol whipped him right there in the hallway. When I hit him, he fell two or three steps down the stairs and the gun slipped out of my hand onto the landing. He started back up the stairs toward me and I kicked him in the throat. This time he fell all the way down to the next landing. These were marble stairs. Between me hitting and kicking him and the fall, he was banged up pretty good.

"In the meantime, one of the neighbors called the police. Dina's brother Larry picked up my gun and took it back into the apartment. When the cops showed up, Dina told them Ronnie was a stalker. One of the cops said there was a report that a gun was involved and wanted to know who had it. Dina told him nobody had a gun.

"Sitting there on the couch, I was getting worried about the gun issue. I knew Larry had hidden it, but it had been in my waistband for so long I figured there was probably a mark from it on my skin. If the cops checked me over, I'd probably be in trouble. They never did, though. Ronnie refused to press charges and they all left. He never bothered her like that again.

"That episode showed Dina another side of me. She knew my reputation on the street and now she knew it was true. She knew her way around, though, and didn't mind. Like I said, we were very much alike. She introduced me to some people in Bensonhurst she knew. They became my friends and, in some cases, my drug-business associates. That was in addition to my contacts in the Persico crew.

"After a while I took Dina to meet my mother and it didn't go all that well. It wasn't that my mother didn't like her. It was just that to my mother, no girl was good enough for me. It didn't matter who the girl was, my mother would find fault with her."

NO-SHOW JOB

Around April, Andrew landed a job that was almost too good to be true. In fact, it wasn't true. Thanks to the Gambino family's influence with labor unions involved in the construction business, he was hired for a job with one basic requirement: Show up only to collect his paycheck.

At that time, major construction was underway at Battery Park City. The Gambinos controlled one of the labor unions with members working there. A deal was worked out where guys from all the crews were hired for the construction jobs. About 10 crew members rotated on and off the payroll at a time.

"My job title was pipe insulator. I was credited with all kinds of overtime and my take-home pay was around a thousand a week. Multiply that by ten guys and you're talking serious money. When I got my paycheck, I took it right to Nicky and signed it over. When he cashed it, he gave me a couple hundred and split the rest with the union guy.

"That wasn't a lot of money for me, but it was free. The best part was that after twenty-six weeks, we got laid off and went on unemployment. Then other crew members were hired to replace us. The unemployment checks were all mine. On top of that, because I was single, they taxed the shit out of me and I got almost all of it back as a tax refund. I think I got a refund of eight or nine thousand and I gave a thousand to Nicky. Not that I had to. It was a way for me to thank him for setting this deal up for me. I don't know if all our guys had the same exact arrangement, but that's the way it worked for me."

PROFIT AND LOSS

Around this time, Andrew got involved in a memorable rebuildable-car episode.

He purchased two Cadillacs that an insurance company was selling as recovered stolen vehicles for about $2,000 each. Their book value was about $20,000 each. Then he stole two cars that were identical right down to the color.

Within a couple of months, he rebuilt both cars. He sold one to a crew member for $13,500, well under book. That gave him a profit of about $11,000 and left the crew member room to make some money when he did an insurance job later on. Andrew helped him strip the car again and he filed an insurance claim. They gave the adjuster a few hundred not to total the Cadillac, just to show damage of around ten thousand. The check from the insurance company was pure profit. After that, they put the car back together and he now had a $20,000 car that cost him only $3,500 out of pocket. Then he sold it at book value and realized $16,000. Between them they made $27,000 on that one car.

"On the downside, the second insurance claim within a year on that Caddy brought me to the attention of an organization I didn't know existed until then. A couple of investigators from the National Auto Theft Bureau showed up at my house. They wanted to know about my car-restoration activities. Did I have receipts for the parts I supposedly bought to rebuild? And why did the cars I was involved with have a habit of having multiple insurance claims filed in short periods of time?"

Ironically, as they sat there talking, the second Caddy was in Andrew's garage, all stripped down. He was doing the same thing with that car as his crewmate had done. He'd paid off the adjuster, filed a claim, and was waiting for the check.

"They finally left, but they made it clear that I was on their radar. Any future insurance claims I was connected to would get a real close going over. That forced me to change my methods. I had enough friends in the business I could work with on a percentage basis without having my name appear on any of the paperwork. So I still made money on insurance fraud, just in a little different manner."

CREDIT-CARD BONANZA

In late 1984, VISA credit-card companies began converting their cards to a hologram format for security purposes. In 1985 and 1986, the new cards were issued to new applicants or as renewals to existing customers. Although the idea behind the new format was to cut down on fraud, for Andrew and his associates, the issuance of the cards opened the door to vast financial rewards. Andrew explained it this way.

"We'd already been making a lot of money off credit cards. But when the companies issued these hologram cards, we made a real killing. I remember that a couple of guys from a Lucchese crew we were friendly with had a meeting with Nicky. I wasn't there, but that same day Nicky told us we had access to thousands of new credit cards with all the related account information.

"Nicky never told us how this all came down. It seemed apparent, though, that the Luccheses had stolen the envelopes containing the new cards from a post office or mail truck. The envelopes contained the cards, personal identification information, and account information that included passwords, PINS, and credit limits.

"Through Nicky's contacts we got stacks of blank New York State driver's licenses. This was just prior to the state issuing photo licenses. We didn't have enough blanks to make a license for every card, but we had a lot of them. That put whoever was using the card in good shape if a merchant requested identification.

"We sold most of the cards to customers for five hundred dollars each. We kept some of them for ourselves too. I knew a lot of merchants who weren't exactly honest. Say I had a card with a three-thousand-dollar limit. I took it to one of them, banged it for twenty-five hundred, and split it with the merchant. The remaining five hundred I used to have fun with, like doing some nightclubbing.

"This scam lasted for several months and we made a killing during that time."

HOSTILE-TAKEOVER ATTEMPT

Late in 1986, Andrew found his lucrative marijuana operation in Utica Park under threat. Another gang evicted Andrew's dealer and claimed the location as its own. This was a challenge that required a swift and firm response.

The new gang was a large group of young Russians who hung around the park at Avenue N and Utica Avenue where Andrew had one of his marijuana dealers. Because he was the only game in town, he was doing $500-$700 a night from there.

"These newcomers didn't know the rules. They didn't know it was my spot and they had to keep their hands off. They told my dealer they were taking over and he had to get out. They even tuned him up a little bit to make their point. Like all things Mafia, this was more than just something between me and them. These kinds of things became known on the streets. People watched to see how the situation was handled. I was trying to expand my operations in that part of town. If I'd have backed down, when the word got around, other people would have challenged me. And it would have reflected badly on the whole crew. Interlopers might figure if I could be pushed around, the rest of the crew was probably soft too. And if I wanted to become a made man in the future, I had to prove I could hold down my territory. For all those reasons, my response had to be fast and decisive.

"The very next day I went to the park with two friends. I had them wait at the entrance, guns in hand, while I went to look for the new drug kingpin, a guy named Ivan. Under my jacket I had a police baton that had been drilled out in the center and filled with lead. Ivan was sitting on a bench with six or seven other guys around. As I approached, they thought I was there to make a buy and asked me what I wanted. I said I wanted to see Ivan, that I heard he had some good stuff. As Ivan got up, I pulled out the baton and hit him on the crown of his head. The sound of the impact was so loud that one of my friends ran over and said, 'Please, Andrew! Don't hit him again. You'll kill him.'

"With Ivan unconscious on the ground, I pulled my gun and told Ivan's boys if I ever saw any of them in the park again, I'd kill them. The next day I flew to Jamaica and stayed for a couple of weeks to let the heat die down. Ivan and his crew never returned to the park."

THE HORSE ROOM

In December 1986, Nicky opened yet another door for Andrew. He asked his underling to learn how to operate one of the horse rooms the crew ran. These betting parlors were the Mob's equivalent of the Off Track Betting (OTB) sites run by the New York State government. They were not only patterned after OTB, they were set up using actual OTB technology and were an important part of the crew's income. Nicky's guys had bribed an OTB cleaning crew to let them into the building at night. They took the computer chip, had it duplicated, then returned it.

"I was real excited when Nicky assigned me to learn the horse room. He had me train in one of the small rooms for a week or so in late December. I liked the job and enjoyed learning it. The place I was working at was run by a girl named Margo. I remember one day that I couldn't work my assigned shift and asked her to switch with me. When I pulled up in my car to go to work, the cops were there and they were taking Margo out in cuffs. I felt so sorry for her, because on a normal day it would have been me under arrest. She took it well, though, and we laughed about it later."

Right after New Year's Day 1987, Nicky put Andrew in one of the bigger OTB operations. It was a great opportunity, but it almost cost him his life.

● ● ●

For Andrew, 1986 had been another successful year financially and personally. Fraudulent automobile, employment, and credit-card deals had generated a lot of money. His drug and shylocking businesses were going strong. And he was being groomed for taking on the additional responsibility of running a horse room. His personal stature had grown over his handling of the attempted takeover of his Utica Park drug operation and he was engaged in a passionate but stormy liaison with Dina. Although his personal relationship with Mike Yannotti was still somewhat strained, professionally they were working well together.

As for the crew, their concerns over the family's direction under John Gotti's leadership never materialized. In fact, Andrew and his crewmates at the street level liked their new boss' blue-collar style. John Gotti was going to be good for business. Or so it seemed.

Gambling and the New York Mob

Gambling accounted for a major portion of the Gambino family's income, as it did for all the New York City crime families. The operations were run by individual crews within each organization and the take often ran into the tens of millions of dollars per year *per crew*. The income was so steady and reliable that Andrew referred to it as "the McDonald's" of the various family enterprises.

The Gambino and Genovese families had the biggest gambling presence and the two sometimes worked together to maximize their returns—there was more than enough to go around.

As usual, to get into the game as an operator, you first had to get permission from the higher-ups. Once permission was granted, the typical arrangement was a 70/30 split, with the bosses taking the 70. There were bonuses for production and a good earner might get a better deal on the split.

In return, the bosses provided the bank and absorbed losses. They also had the connections for sports-betting "lay-offs" when necessary. (In the world of sports bookmaking, the house tries to avoid having too big a position on one side of a game in order to keep its risk in check. So if a side gets too much action, the bookie looks for ways to bet some of it with other bookies, which is known as "laying off.")

The operators did the work and assumed the physical risk of running the games. They were on what's known as a "make-up" with the bosses, which meant that while they didn't have to cover losses when they occurred, they also couldn't take any money out of future winnings until the losses were recouped.

Andrew's introduction to the world of organized-crime gambling was a new experience for him. He understood gambling and was fast with numbers. Still, he had to learn the ropes, which he did working in the Gambino off-track-betting parlor and from other operators, such as the boss of a family-run crap game dating back to the 1970s.

CRAPS

Craps was one of the most popular and lucrative gambling options organized crime offered. The Gambinos ran their game six days a week. In order to participate, a gambler had to either be known to the operator or vouched for by a known player.

Although the action took place at various sites, the method by which gamblers got to the games was always the same. A player first showed up at 129 Mott Street. From there he was taken by a Gambino-provided shuttle to wherever the game was being held that night.

Of course, these measures were in place for security. Surprisingly, there was almost no payoff (known as "pad") to law enforcement, so the games had to be protected from raids conducted by the "morals squad," the arm of the NYPD that tried to find and shut down the illegal casinos. The venues changed all the time, which is where the name "floating crap game" comes from. When the police did raid a game, they wrecked the venue and confiscated the money. The consequences for the operators were most serious if they were caught with $10,000 or more in their possession (a felony).

To avoid this, the bank was kept off-premises and money was continually shipped out of the location as it was won from the players.

Contrary to what's often portrayed in movies and on TV, the games weren't held in dingy back rooms. Rather, they tended to be in high-profile "social clubs," where a lot of activity didn't look out of place.

So a lot of steps were taken to protect the games, but at the same time, there was always a question about how much the local law really cared, as Andrew explains.

"In the early eighties, President Ronald Reagan was coming to New York City and one of his arranged stops was a restaurant called Angelo's that was located on Mulberry Street in the heart of Manhattan's Little Italy. A few days before his arrival, the Secret Service, along with local police captains, reached out to a Genovese-family wise guy named Sammy 'Meatballs' Aparo, along with two other capos from the Gambinos, and asked them to 'please' close down the crap games until the president's trip was over. Everyone accommodated the request and the games were closed for two days. But after that, both families assumed that not only did the local authorities have a pretty good idea about the size and locations of the crap games, but maybe even the Secret Service knew, too."

With rare exceptions, the New York game had betting limits designed to protect the house from suffering major losses to a hot roll. The normal betting cap was $300. Sometimes that was raised to $500, depending on the players and the mood and bankroll of the operators.

The house started a $300-limit game with a bank of around $30,000. When higher limits were in effect, the bank was in the area of $100,000. Unless high rollers made arrangements for a special game, they were held to the limits no matter how much money they had in their pockets. But that didn't mean they couldn't play higher.

To satisfy those who craved more action, players could bet directly with one another without going through the house. This was pure "street craps," where one player "faded" another's action. If a shooter wanted to bet $500 on a game with a $300 limit, he could offer the extra $200 to whomever was willing to book the action. Once he had a fader, that portion of the wager was strictly between the players; the house had no financial interest in the outcome of those bets either way.

This side action was often booked at negotiated terms, but only the uninitiated "squares" would accept a bet at diminished odds. For the most part, the players in these games knew their stuff and understood dice probabilities cold. Hence, it was far more likely for man-to-man bets above the limit to be covered at correct odds.

"It wasn't uncommon for a guy with money looking for action to lay two grand to win a grand on the four or ten, which was an even bet for both players," says Andrew. "They didn't care about getting an edge. They just wanted to gamble high."

Another difference in the underground dice games was that most of the customers were "wrong bettors," meaning they bet on the "don't" side of the layout. It's the opposite in legal casinos, where almost everyone bets the pass line, or the "do" side. There was a good reason for betting wrong in the underground game: better odds.

The version of the game played in the legal casinos is what the gangsters call "Western craps." That's not the game the Gambino family ran. Their game was a derivative known as "New York craps." The two are similar in many respects, but have major differences as well. The man who ran the games for the Gambinos believes those differences made his offering more player-friendly.

The biggest difference was in the basic pass and don't pass bets, which aren't even called that in New York craps.

Instead, there was a bet called "Win or Lose." Betting Win worked exactly like a pass line bet in the standard game. And betting Lose was similar to a bet on don't pass, with one major difference—there were no "barred" numbers.

In the legal-casino game of craps, on the "come-out" roll, don't pass bettors lose on a 7 or 11 and win on a 2 or 3, but only tie if a 12 is rolled. It's called "barring the 12" and it's the way the house gets its 1.4% edge against the don'ts. If they didn't bar the 12, the don't bettors would enjoy the same 1.4% advantage that the house does against pass-line bettors. Incredibly, this was the case in New York craps (and the reason most bet on the don't side). There was a saying, "Right bettors go broke; wrong bettors go on vacation."

"How could we do it and still make a profit? It was human nature," Andrew insists. "The limits on the Win or Lose bets were set well below the limits on the other bets—usually a hundred dollars. Also, there were no come or don't come options, so there was no way to get more action unless you made one of the other bets, all of which carried a house advantage. Everyone did, of course. The Win and Lose bets were the ultimate loss leader."

"You say it makes no sense?" added Andrew's mentor, who dealt New York craps for decades. "The guys didn't like the bar twelve, so we took it out. We made millions of dollars year after year dealing the game just like that."

The heart of the game was the "boxes," which displayed the point numbers 4, 5, 6, 8, 9, and 10. You could "place" or "lay" the numbers at any time and this is where most of the action was. Here, too, the deal was better for the player than in standard casino craps. For example, laying against the numbers in a legal casino yields a casino edge of between 2.4% and 4%, while in New York craps, the edges ranged between 1.64% and 2.44%. Why play in Vegas?

Another variation was that hardway bets were only good for one roll. A one-roll hardway, known as a "hop," carries a higher house edge than a standard hardway. And since the outcome is determined in a single roll, this policy induced the gamblers to make more bets at a higher vig, thus earning the house more profit.

But other than hardway hops, the odds in New York craps were better for the players. They had to be, because of the general level of sophistication and mathematical competence of their customers. The mob's crap customers weren't dummies.

And the games were generally clean. Andrew knows of instances where a dealer switched in gaffed dice, but that was rare. Math and human nature were enough to get the money at dice and there was a certain reverence for craps that didn't exist for cards and other games.

"These players wanted to shoot craps," Andrew says. "They didn't play blackjack or poker on the side. They were there to bet on dice the way they had all their lives, so for the most part, we had to keep the games pure."

The dealers came from everywhere and the talent pool was surprisingly rich. Some had dealt craps in the legal casinos of Atlantic City or Vegas, but most had simply grown up around the game and could deal it in their sleep.

If a player tapped out and needed money to get back in the game, no problem. The operator was responsible for having a shylock on site to make loans. Call it the Gambinos' version of today's ATM machines.

Interestingly, booze was never available during the game. A lunch was served before play started and a waitress was on hand to deliver beverages, but it was strictly non-alcoholic.

The daughter of a man who owned one of the buildings the Gambinos rented to run their games became a federal prosecutor years later. In an ironic side note, she vigorously went after the very men whose money her father probably used to put her through law school.

CARDS

Another good money maker for the Gambinos was running card games. Card gatherings were different from craps. These games targeted outsiders and *how* they got the money was less of an issue than simply getting it.

In poker, the house made its profit the traditional way, by raking the pot. They took 5% of the money bet on every hand and the earn from just one big-money game could reach several thousand dollars.

Although raking a percentage from poker didn't involve cheating, blackjack was a different story. Blackjack games were much more like what you might expect (fear) from mob-run gambling. The games were dealt from 4- or 6-deck shoes and employed Vegas rules for the most part. But the rules didn't really matter—the shoes the Gambino operators used to deal their blackjack games weren't designed with the players' best interests in mind.

One was called a "mirrored shoe." As the name implies, this gizmo allowed the dealer to see what cards were about to be dealt before they came out, knowledge that was clearly beneficial to a master card manipulator.

The "tap 5" shoe was a man-made miracle for a dealer prone to getting the dreaded 16 hand on the deal. It could also be the death knell for a player who'd doubled down. A simple tap on the shoe automatically caused a 5 to appear as the next card. Players with a 19 or 20, or those who'd doubled or split pairs based on the dealer having a 6 up, watched a seemingly unconscious dealer routinely turn those nasty 15s and 16s into 20s and 21s time after time.

Andrew offers one example of how powerful the crooked blackjack dealers were. "This guy named Al ran weekly Las Vegas nights out of a synagogue. Every week Al got his clock cleaned on his blackjack tables. Finally, he hired cheats to deal for him. He paid out thirty percent of the take. Real quick, Al recouped his losses and was turning a hefty profit. Once Al was back on his feet, the cheats asked that their cut be raised to sixty percent. Al refused. But that turned out to be an unwise business decision. The card mechanics moved on and Al went back to losing."

Limits in these games were high—$25-$2,000 was typical—because the cheating insulated the crew from risk. But the devices were used only against strangers—the majority of whom tended to be Asian.

Andrew emphasizes this point. "Pretty much a hundred percent of the blackjack were swindle games that targeted high-rolling strangers. No friends or associates were allowed to participate, because this was strictly a robbery."

SPORTS BETTING

Though not as venerable as craps, booking sports held a high position in the mob's gambling pantheon. Sports betting has always been among gambling's most restricted (by the government) activities, while simultaneously being something that millions of sports enthusiasts love to do. That made it a natural for operators of underground games.

"Betting with bookies is the same as betting in a sports book in Las Vegas," Andrew explains, "only easier. When working with our bookies, the customer didn't have to show up in person to make a bet. Instead, he was assigned a number and we handled the transactions over the phone. The customer called in to a central office" [these operations were referred to as "sports offices" rather than sports books], "identify his bookie, give his number, and place the bet."

When he was making book, Andrew used the name "Sonny." A call to the office from one of his customers might go something like this. "This is for Sonny twenty-seven. I'll take the Redskins plus seven over the Giants for one-ten."

That meant he was Sonny's customer number 27 and he

was betting $110 that the Washington Redskins would either beat the New York Giants outright or lose by less than seven points. It was the standard bet-$110-to-win-$100 arrangement, same as it is in a legal Nevada sports book.

The Gambino bookmaking operation offered most sports—NFL, college football and basketball, NBA, MLB, boxing matches, etc. They dealt sides, totals, parlays, teasers, and other betting options, but no futures *ever* (that required accounting and the holding of money, the sorts of things that could lead to disputes). Limits were high—up to $5,000 on sides and $2,000 on totals, more than many Las Vegas books will take today. The opening lines came from several sources, including the famous "Vegas line" that originated out of the Stardust.

"When the office received a call," Andrew explains, "we first checked the player's 'sheet' to see how much credit he had. If his bet didn't put him over his credit limit, we took his action."

Credit was an integral part of the sports-betting puzzle. The guys manning the office updated the customer's information after each game, so his credit situation was always current going into the next round of action. A player could get as much credit as the bosses thought he was worth and good for.

"They constantly monitored a guy's action and followed his betting and borrowing patterns. For example, if someone was going on a losing streak, they knew the average of his prior bets and how much credit he usually carried. If he was all of a sudden betting more and losing, they intervened. Keep in mind that seven out of ten of our customers were people from the neighborhood and we knew their backgrounds and financial capabilities. We knew what most of them could afford.

"As a rule of thumb, when a guy owed, we allowed him to play for cash if he wanted to. If he won, we took a piece toward what he owed when he cashed out. We worked with these guys, because getting heavy over a debt usually meant losing a customer that you knew would have money again and would find somewhere else to bet. Then you'd have to chase that money. Our method worked very well. Now, if a customer ran away with a big tab, we definitely tracked him down, because at that point, he was outright robbing us."

Although bets were taken by phone, there still had to be personal contact between the bookie and his customers to settle up. This was done once a week on Tuesdays when the bookie drove around and met with his clients. Why Tuesday?

"Collecting on Tuesday gave the gamblers the chance to finish off their betting week with the 'Monday Night Football' game. Players on a losing streak over the weekend loved to use the Monday game to try to recoup. It worked, sometimes. But just as often, trying to get even plunged the losers even deeper into debt. Then we'd monitor them. And there was no shortage of shylocks around in case a gambler needed a quick influx of cash to pay us off."

If a bookie was getting too much action on a team, he laid off some of those bets to other books. That spread the risk around, so no individual bookie had to absorb a devastating loss. The families preferred to keep the money within their own operations, but they'd go outside to the shops of other families if necessary. Here, too, it was friendly business in the greater interests of keeping the money flowing for everyone.

When Andrew was operating, there wasn't a strong connection to Las Vegas. That changed a few years later. In the late '80s and early '90s, coinciding with technological breakthroughs in communication devices (such as pagers and cell phones), it became expedient and efficient to use the Vegas books for the layoff. Certain guys with heavy Eastern accents all of a sudden became staples in various Sin City sports books (this was a big factor in the enactment of the "messenger-betting" rules that banned cell phones from the books until 2009).

Just like in Nevada, the bookies also moved the point spread on a game that posed a potential problem, in order to encourage customers to bet the other way. If the action on that game could be brought into balance, it mitigated the risk of a financial disaster.

Moving the point spreads was also a tactic used against winning players. In the business, this is known as dealing a "double line." It means offering one line to the public, because you know they'll take the worst of a number shaded against popular teams, and another to the wise guys who'd take advantage of that shading, if you let them, by betting the other way. Many offshore sports books employ this practice today.

"We treated the winners well," Andrew says. "But if they were too good, we fucked up their lines. This wasn't Vegas; we could change the line instantly when we needed to. But we never chased a winner. By that I mean we never punished a winner by shutting him out or telling him to go elsewhere."

RACE BETTING

The race-betting business was also run out of the sports office. Horses drew far less action than sports, but it was a good earner. The mob's payouts were better than the competition's, which was the New York Off-Track Betting parlors; to pay their costs, the OTBs took out too much. So players could get more on winning tickets from the illegal joints.

"We took a lot of business away from the OTBs," says Andrew. "We offered food and had the same simulcast live feeds showing mostly every racetrack in the country. We extended small amounts of credit to good customers and offered a twenty-five-percent kickback on the weekly loss, because these guys were never gonna win. As the proverb goes, 'All horse bettors die broke and live with broken shoes.'"

People like Andrew, who booked through Nick Corozzo's horse rooms, worked on a percentage basis. They received 25% of the profits on winning weeks, while Corozzo paid all the losses and put the operators on a make-up until they got the losses back. But losing weeks were the exception and not the rule in the Gambino-controlled sports- and race-betting venues. Andrew never experienced one and his peers were in the black the vast majority of the time.

NUMBERS

The illegal numbers game—also known as a "policy racket"—is a very simple proposition. The bettor picks three single-digit numbers. If they match the "daily number" announced the following day, he's a winner.

In the early days, numbers betting was run almost exclusively by black gangsters. Like any lottery, the low cost of entry made the game extremely popular in poor, mostly black, neighborhoods, which meant that almost everyone was a potential customer.

Eventually, white organized criminals in New York took an interest in the business. The Genovese crime family got involved first and the other families followed.

Under the Gambino rules, winners were paid 500-1. So a 50¢ bet returned $250. Since the true odds of hitting were closer to 1,000-1, the numbers gave the operators a healthy edge (they kept about half of whatever was bet).

The daily number was (and still is) derived from the total handle at a specified local racetrack. "If a person bet with a Gambino store," Andrew says, "there were two daily numbers in play: the New York number and the Brooklyn number. The New York number came from the results of the third, fifth, and seventh races at the designated track. The Brooklyn number resulted from the last three digits of the total mutuel handle at whichever track was being used."

There were other ways of doing it. Some unaffiliated numbers operators in Westchester County used the "1-in-the-middle" method when computing their payoffs. Under that system, if the winning set of numbers had a 1 in the middle, the winners were paid at a rate of only 300-1 rather than the normal 500.

As in any free market, the public eventually decides what they'll "pay" for anything, and the Gambinos reasoned that they made plenty by paying out extra. As a result, their game thrived and by the time Andrew became active, the numbers racket was a big part of the family's gambling income. Nick Corozzo operated several games in his territory.

The pay structure for the Gambino stores worked as follows. The store's boss—called the "controller"—received 600-1 on winning bets. This assured that he'd make a profit even on customer wins. In addition, the crew boss paid the controller 35% of the business' take. From that, the controller kept 10% and paid the runner—the guy who took the bets and collected and paid out the money—the balance, which equaled 25% of the total take. The boss kept all the rest, minus 3%-4% for the cost of paperwork.

"One well-known numbers store in New York City did around three hundred thousand in business every week. He passed all his action off to the two biggest numbers runners in the city for ten percent, then collected thirty grand or so a week while the runners did all the work," Andrew recalls.

When New York City started its own lottery, it paid the merchants selling the tickets only 6%. That was 4% less than organized crime paid its store operators. And if the legal lottery was getting too much action on a particular number, it shut down that number. The illegal competition didn't do that. Hence, the numbers rackets were able to continue operating even after the lottery was created.

As Andrew likes to point out, state and local governments frequently open businesses with which organized crime has had financial success. Horse betting produced a lot of money and New York opened Off-Track-Betting parlors. Numbers games took in tons of money and state lotteries came into being.

LAS VEGAS

It's well-known that organized crime has a long history in Las Vegas. Over the years, many families made money on their Sin City ventures. For the Chicago Outfit and its partners in Kansas City, Milwaukee, and Cleveland, and for the New York families, Las Vegas served as a cash cow for decades.

The New York families had their hands deep in the Vegas pie. In the late 1960s and 1970s, the Genovese family, for example, had interests in Caesars Palace, the Sands, and the Tropicana. They sent their guys out to Vegas to work as dealers and cashiers and to serve as "connections" for visiting mobsters and their associates.

For as long as they had their people in place, the New Yorkers also participated in the "skim." The purloined cash was transported across the country by a legendary female courier. For obvious reasons, her identity, the details of her visits to Vegas, and her modes of transportation were highly secretive, but the cash always arrived without incident. Back in New York, the money went straight to the Genovese family, which functioned as the banker for all five families.

The mob tolerated nothing that might upset the financial apple cart. One good example was that New York wise guys who left Las Vegas without settling up their gambling debts had to answer directly to Genovese boss Anthony "Fat Tony" Salerno himself. Because of that, the Vegas casinos rarely got stiffed on New York markers.

Of course, connected gamblers weren't without certain perks. Andrew remembers the tale of a Lucchese associate who arranged credit for Mob-connected visitors.

"A visitor approached the Lucchese guy, identified himself, and asked for a credit line of, say twenty Gs. The Lucchese guy took the visitor to the cage, which verified he was who he said he was and was good for the money. If everything checked out okay, a marker was approved.

"If the player lost the twenty grand, he got together with the Lucchese guy to settle up. At that time, he was offered a special deal: fifty percent off his debt to settle up in cash before he left. It was an offer that couldn't be refused. They went back to the cage, where the borrower paid the ten grand, which was split between the fixer and his cashier confederate. Then the marker was ripped up and it was as if it never existed. Everybody was happy—except for the casino, which didn't see a dime."

With the corporate takeover of the Las Vegas casinos, combined with technological advancements, the days of organized-crime skimming from the count rooms and cashier cages are gone. However, clever crooks can still take advantage of the casinos. It involves the new extension of the gambling industry: offshore betting.

The reliability of telephonic communications and computer technology has made it possible for gaming entrepreneurs to open businesses in places such as Costa Rica with minimal overhead expenses. Initially, these cyber-bookmakers and their customers escaped the tax burdens and other laws associated with gambling on United States soil. However, the U.S. government is now aggressively pursuing them and attempting to close the loopholes—legal and otherwise—that make offshore betting so appealing.

In addition to tax breaks, other features of online wagering appeal to some gamblers. The offshores offer the convenience of doing business on the Internet or by an 800 phone number. Money doesn't have to be tendered (though it may have already been "posted up" and be on account) when the bet is placed. And most of these businesses offer their customers various financial incentives, usually in the form of sign-up bonuses. For example, a customer who funds an account with $1,000 might get an extra $200, for a total of $1,200.

If you walk into any major Las Vegas casino today, look around the sports book for a guy with a laptop computer (patrons are allowed to bring computers into the casino) and wearing a Bluetooth headset. He may very well be a cyberbookie. He has customers meet him in the casino's own betting parlor to take their action. He can service his customers while monitoring the latest line changes. He can even enjoy some free casino beverages if he's so inclined.

Sports betting is legal in Vegas, so why wouldn't the gambler just go to the window in the casino's sports book to make his bet? Because he'd have to come up with the money to make the wager.

Like the Gambino-run books, the cyber-bookies' betting cycle lasts a week. At the end of the cycle, the bettor can settle his account online through the use of a credit card or meet personally with his local "agent" to balance the books.

Running an offshore betting business was so lucrative that it appealed greatly to Nick Corozzo and he opened one himself. However, it was a decision that contributed to his eventual downfall.

9

1987

In the early part of 1987, Andrew was presented with the chance to move to a larger horse parlor located on Stillwell Avenue in Bensonhurst. It was an opportunity he welcomed, but it turned out to be fraught with danger as well.

This particular site consisted of two rooms on the ground floor of an eight-family apartment building that had previously been a Mob social club. The satellite, mounted on the roof, was invisible from street level. It could only be seen from passing subway trains running on the elevated tracks.

The betting parlor operated daily from about eight in the morning until 11 or so at night. The main room sat around 50 people comfortably and accommodated 100 or so for special events like the Kentucky Derby if some were willing to stand. Four large-screen televisions, three showing different racetracks and the fourth various other sporting events, ran continuously during business hours.

It was a customer-friendly environment with food and non-alcoholic drinks provided to the bettors for free. They were served by a waitress who worked for a salary plus tips. In addition, customers who wanted to partake in other games of chance could play poker or bet on the daily lottery number, with a percentage of the action going into the Mob's coffers.

A second much smaller room was the manager's office. This is where the bets were actually taken and all the digital equipment was kept. As Andrew explains, the financial side of the business was tilted somewhat in favor of the gangsters.

"Thanks to the stolen OTB computer chip, we ran our horse parlors pretty much as OTB ran theirs. The main difference was that we didn't pay out quite the same as OTB. We didn't pay track odds on bets like daily doubles and trifectas. If those bets hit at full odds, it could have hurt us bad, so we shaved them a little to our advantage. We did pay track odds on win, place, and show bets, as well as exactas.

"I ended up on Stillwell Avenue because Nicky asked me to give Joey, the guy running the place, a hand. Joey was like a godson to Nicky and was in his mid-forties then. But in reality there was more behind this than just helping Joey out. You see, organized crime is rife with nepotism. The bosses like to take care of their sons, brothers, nephews, cousins, and godsons by giving them positions within the organization with a chance to earn at least some authority. Of course, the people getting those jobs aren't necessarily qualified to do them.

"In this case, Nicky was concerned about Joey. He knew Joey was drinking heavily, possibly skimming, and not running things with the family's best interests in mind. So I wasn't sent there just to help out. I was also there to observe and see what Joey was up to.

"When I first showed up, I wasn't sure how Joey would take it. He was no dummy and had to suspect I was Nicky's eyes and ears. But he treated me well and taught me the business side of the operation. We worked well together and before long developed a thriving business. Each week we were tens of thousands of dollars in the blue [on the plus side]. The overall volume of business tripled. We treated the customers like gold, feeding them well and sometimes making small loans to those in need. Things were going so well I even started to think of Joey as my friend.

"Nicky noticed the improvement in the profits. And he wasn't the only one. John Gotti himself commented about it. His brother Gene was one of our best customers and saw first-hand how we ran the place and the business we were doing."

But for Andrew and Joey, the honeymoon period came to an end within a few months, when Joey's bad habits caught up with him. His alcohol problem got worse and affected his health. He became undependable, constantly taking days off or going home early. It all came to a head one day when Andrew was working and looking forward to his day off.

"That night I had to take Joey the money for the next day's opening bank. I was on my way to meet him at a bar down the street from our social club on East Ninety-third and Avenue L. As I passed the club, I saw Nicky standing outside and pulled over to say hello. He asked me to give him a ride home. On the way, I stopped at the bar and took Joey's money in, twelve thousand dollars, as I recall. Nicky waited in the car. Joey was feeling no pain and was mushing it up with some broad. I gave him the money and left.

"About seven the next morning, Joey called me and wanted to know when I'm gonna drop off the bank. I asked him what the hell he was talking about. I'd given him the money last night. Then he told me to stop fucking around and bring him the money or there was going to be trouble. I told him to go fuck himself and hung up. About five minutes later Nicky's son-in-law Scotty called. He said to get over to the luncheonette right away because Nicky wanted to see me.

"When I walked into the diner, the whole crew was there staring at me. Joey started right off with, 'Where's the money, kid? You think you can rob us and get away with it?'

"I started laughing and told Joey to screw himself. Nicky had been with me and knew the truth. I was waiting for him to step forward. But he kept quiet and let Joey talk, digging himself a deeper hole. Finally, Nicky jumped up and grabbed Joey by the shirt. He said, 'You motherfucker. I was with the kid last night when he dropped off the goddamn money.'

"Joey's face turned white and I thought he was going to faint. And then he started to cry and told how the girl he was with at the bar had rolled him. She took the money, all of it. He had been too ashamed to admit it so he made up the story that I never brought the money to him. Nicky said, 'You're lucky you're a relative or I'd let the kid kill you right here.'

"I would have killed the bastard, too. The Mob doesn't take internal theft lightly. If I hadn't given Nicky that ride home, my body would probably have ended up in a landfill or in the trunk of an abandoned car.

"But Joey and I both walked out of the luncheonette alive. His punishment was exclusion from all crew businesses. My reward was that I was made the sole manager of the Stillwell Avenue horse room.

"Business continued to boom. To some guys it became a home away from home. We had such crowds every day that sometimes the beat cops would knock on the door and ask that the people who were double- or triple-parked move their cars. The only reason I can think of that they didn't try to shut us down is that they thought it was just a social club.

"Pretty soon I was fencing stolen property too. Guys started coming in to get rid of hot jewelry, mink coats, televisions, weapons, and audio equipment. You name it, they brought it. Some days I was able to pocket thousands of dollars without leaving my chair."

With all that money rolling in, Andrew took certain precautions to protect it from the law and limit his liability in the event of a raid.

"I had two places close by that I used to stash money when I thought we had too much cash on hand. One was two doors down at a deli my friend owned. The other was an apartment I kept a couple of blocks away. By keeping a relatively small amount on the premises, we wouldn't lose it all in the event of a pinch. And the charges if I got arrested were more serious the higher the amount of money seized. So I kept a smaller bank, but the money was close enough that I could get it fast if somebody hit a big win.

"The success of the horse room earned me a nickname from Nicky. Every time I reported to him the profits were soaring, so he started calling me 'Good News.'"

EVERYBODY WALKS

Andrew wasn't the only one Nicky Corozzo heard good news from early in the year. On March 13, four days before his 47th birthday, he received an early present. A jury acquitted him of the federal racketeering charges for which he had been indicted in 1985. Nicky's six remaining co-defendants, including John Gotti, also left the courtroom as free men. Everybody walked. The government's case, which had once seemed so strong, had failed to produce a single guilty verdict.

Leading up to and during the trial, Gotti had predicted that very outcome. That confident forecast could have been made by an innocent man who trusted the criminal-justice system or perhaps one with great faith in the abilities of his lawyer. However, in this case, another option seems more likely. Gotti had reason to believe that at the worst, the trial would end in a hung jury.

As the jurors left the courtroom, Gotti, the other defendants, their lawyers, and supporters gave them a standing ovation. As Gotti was heading for the door, a reporter asked him how he and his associates were able to prevail. Gotti pointed to the now-empty jury box and said, "With these people here." But it may have been more appropriate had he said, "Thanks to Mr. Pape."

George H. Pape was the jury foreman for the 1987 trial. On February 24, 1992, after years of rumor and speculation that Gotti had inside help in his string of victories over government prosecutors, Mr. Pape was indicted for selling his vote and exerting influence on the other jurors to vote in Gotti's favor. He'd collected $60,000 for his services.

In Pape's subsequent trial, Mob turncoat Sammy Gravano provided crucial testimony on behalf of the government regarding the Mob's arrangement with Pape to assure there would not be a conviction. Pape was convicted and sentenced to three years in prison. But although the acquittal may have been tainted, it was an acquittal nonetheless.

ALLIANCES

Over time, Andrew had his share of problems with members of crews from other crime families, particularly the Gaspipe Casso faction of the Luccheses. However, he also developed friendships or at least working relationships with others. And contrary to what some may believe, associating or committing crimes with members of other families didn't violate Mob protocol. There was one caveat, though, as Andrew explains.

"If you wanted to commit crimes with guys from another family it was okay. But you had to remember one thing. At the end of the day, your loyalty had to be with your own crew and family. When I was out there earning with these guys, I had to make sure I kicked some of the money up to Nicky. And if trouble ever broke out between crews or factions, my loyalty was to Nicky and nobody else."

Andrew conducted his various business ventures according to that rule. Nicky received financial benefits from all of Andrew's endeavors. And if push ever came to shove, Andrew's gun would be on Nicky's side.

Because it was all about making money, Andrew sometimes did business with individuals he didn't like. One example was his involvement with Robert, a drug dealer associated with the Teddy Persico crew of the Colombo family.

"This Robert was kind of an asshole. I didn't like him and neither did Mike Yannotti. But he had connections at Kennedy Airport for drugs to be flown in—I believe they originated in Arizona. When the drugs got to Kennedy, Robert's people set them aside for him to pick up. They were making a fortune and I made a deal with Robert to get in on the action. It was a good marriage, but it only lasted a few months.

"In June I got a phone call in the middle of the night saying that Mike Yannotti had been involved in a shooting at a club called the Player's Lounge. It was a Colombo hangout and some of the Gambinos went there, including Sammy Gravano's Bensonhurst crew.

"I don't know exactly what caused it, but on this particular night, there was an altercation between Mike and Robert. Later that night, they found Robert in his car in a parking lot at Caesar's Bay Bazaar on Shore Parkway. He was bleeding from multiple gunshot wounds. He was in bad shape for a while, but he survived.

"The next day Mike Yannotti called me. We still had that rivalry thing going in our personal relationship. When it came to business, though, we were a team. Mike admitted that he'd shot Robert. And then he told me that I was spending all my time at the horse room or with the other guys I'd become involved with in the drug operation. He said he could use my help and I needed to spend more time with him and my own crew. He asked me to keep away from the Colombos until the dust cleared over Robert's shooting. That would happen after Teddy Persico and Nicky had a sit-down [a personal meeting] to resolve the matter. I said okay.

"Next we talked about what we'd do if there were any repercussions over the shooting before Teddy and Nicky got together. We were particularly concerned about this kid Frank

Smith who worked for Teddy. He was a stone-cold shooter. He'd kill you in a minute. So in case Frank or anybody came after Mike, we made plans for how we'd dispose of them.

"My loyalty was to Mike and helping him was the right thing to do. It cost me big, though. I went from making up to eight thousand a week, split between me and two associates, to making nothing. Those things happened. I know that I put a lot of pressure on my friends at times too. I asked them to do things that probably hurt them financially. But that's the way it was.

"Eventually, Teddy and Nicky had their sit-down and everything was squashed. But you don't just come back from being shot and forget about it. Robert didn't; he held a grudge. We'd see each other from time to time. When we did, we'd talk. But I was always aware of my surroundings and knew that I'd never be able to get careless around Robert or his friends."

In an interesting coincidence, two other men were shot and killed the same night Mike Yannotti shot Robert. Their names were Eddie and Vincent Carini. The Carini brothers were also associated with the Colombos. They were notorious killers and hung around with the equally dangerous Frank Smith. Andrew explains the story behind their murders.

"In 1986 Carmine Persico was convicted on federal racketeering charges and sentenced to life plus thirty-nine years in prison. The following March he sent word to his crew that he wanted a federal prosecutor named William Aronwald killed. The order to set up the hit went to Joel Cacace, who was also known as Joe Waverly. Cacace assigned the Carini brothers and Frank Smith to handle it.

"Supposedly, Cacace wrote the name Aronwald on a slip of paper and gave it to the Carinis and Smith. But they made a mistake and killed the guy's father instead. He was an administrative law judge who handled parking tickets. He had nothing to do with prosecuting organized crime. As punishment for botching the hit, Cacace had the Carini brothers murdered three months later. They were found dead in separate cars on a block in Sheepshead Bay the same night Mike Yannotti did Robert. It was a bad night for the Colombos."

For unknown reasons, Frank Smith didn't make Cacace's hit list. But apparently fearing for his life and having fallen out of favor with the Colombos, Smith later became a government witness. Andrew believes he knows exactly why the killer turned on his colleagues.

"Frank did a lot of work [shootings] for the Colombos. He was loyal to them and even took a fifteen-year sentence for a crime he didn't commit to protect somebody else. He served every day of it and kept his mouth shut. His thanks was that while he was away, his crew gave his family no support. When he asked them for help, they ignored him. And when he asked to be released from the Colombos to join a Lucchese family crew, they said no. Eventually, Frank learned the same lessons I did: that in organized crime, the bosses demand loyalty and respect from the bottom up. It's a one-way street; it doesn't come from the top down. They expect the street guys to take it on the chin for the team. But when a soldier needs their support, it's not there. The bosses of today treat their people like shit and then they can't understand it when somebody flips. I've got news for them. What goes around comes around."

As for Joel Cacace, on August 13, 2004, he pleaded guilty to racketeering charges. He admitted his role in the Aronwald murder and was sentenced to 20 years in prison.

ANOTHER ROBERT

Not all of Andrew's pals were criminals. Gilbert was one of his closest legitimate friends. In the late summer Gilbert was having problems with Robert Arena, a member of the Domenico "Danny" Cutaia crew of the Lucchese family. Gilbert had been summoned to meet with Arena. Fearing he might be in danger, he asked Andrew to accompany him.

Andrew knew Arena from the neighborhood. He was a couple of years younger than Andrew and stood well over six feet and weighed around 250 pounds. Not intimidated by Arena's size or affiliations, Andrew agreed to go to the meeting with Gilbert.

When they arrived at the meeting location, Andrew waited in the car as Gilbert and Arena met on the street. Almost immediately, Arena started to punch Gilbert. Andrew left the car and walked toward the combatants. He describes what happened next.

"Robert noticed me approaching them. He turned toward me and smiled, then he gave me a big hug and a kiss on the cheek. He asked me how I'd been, what was going on, and what was the matter. I told him Gilbert was my friend and I couldn't let this happen. I said I didn't know what this thing was all about and I wasn't saying who was right or wrong. I just didn't want my friend hurt.

"Robert said it wasn't anything that couldn't be worked out. He was just pissed off, because he thought Gilbert was acting like a punk. Robert and I took a walk and talked things over. When we passed his car, a couple of his friends were inside. The father of one of them was a captain in the Gambino family. We talked for a while and then went back to Gilbert and him and Robert talked. Things got worked out right then and there were no more problems between them. Robert and me became fast friends from that point forward."

● ● ●

Around September or October, Andrew learned from Dina that he was going to be a father. The news was exciting at the time. But looking back at it now, Andrew questions whether people like him should want wives and children.

"It was selfish for a guy like me to want a family of my own. I couldn't be there for them, because I was married to the crime family. I think the only reason guys like me want to get married or have kids is to be able to fit in with the normal society. But I wasn't thinking like that back then."

As Andrew prepared to start his third year as a member of Nicky's crew, he began to think of where he wanted his career to take him. But he didn't know then that his encounter with Ralph Burzo on East 2nd Street was only months away. And he hadn't yet learned his lessons about Mob politics and loyalty. However, his education would soon begin when he got into trouble and Nicky Corozzo's support wasn't quite what he expected.

For Andrew, winds of change were on the way.

10

1988

At some point during their working years, most people take stock of where they are and where they want to go with their careers. Although he didn't have what the majority of us would consider to be a normal job, Andrew was striving to be a professional in his chosen field, so he had work-related decisions to make. As he improved his criminal skills and became more valuable to his boss, he started thinking about a step up the career ladder. In his case, that meant becoming a made man.

Traditionally, to become a made member of the Mafia, the inductee had to be of full Italian or Sicilian descent. However, to become a made man in the Italian-American Mafia today, the candidate must only be of half-Italian descent on either his father's or mother's side, provided he has an Italian surname. A frequent example of a made member who wasn't a full-blooded Italian is John A. "Junior" Gotti, whose mother was of Russian and Jewish descent. However, with a person as powerful as his father behind him, the traditional requirement was waived.

And the nominee should also have "made his bones" by committing a murder on behalf of his Mafia family or crew. Many Mafia families, especially the more violent factions, don't consider a killing for personal reasons to meet this requirement.

If a man does get made, his elevated status entitles him to additional respect and financial rewards. In addition, he is not allowed to be killed without the permission of the Mob hierarchy—in essence, making him untouchable to his organized-crime rivals or enemies.

Andrew believed he had a legitimate shot at becoming a full member of the Gambinos in spite of his youth. He was qualified in regard to his ancestry. He'd demonstrated his loyalty and his ability as an earner who would do whatever it took to protect his turf. And even though he hadn't yet committed murder for Nicky, it wasn't for a lack of willingness to pull the trigger when necessary. He didn't think he was someone special, but that he was as deserving as the others in his crew. Besides, as Andrew describes the made-man issue as he knows it, the rules and requirements of tradition weren't always adhered to.

"People hear a lot of things about being made that sound good, but just aren't true in the real world. For example, made men aren't supposed to be involved in drug dealing. You've gotta kill somebody to get made. Everybody who gets made has been there and done that. They won't tell their men to do anything they haven't done themselves. That's all bullshit. The human element involved makes some of these so-called rules a joke.

"Does anyone really think organized crime doesn't make a huge amount of money from the drug business? I was involved in dealing pot and shook down dealers of hard drugs. I kicked money to Nicky and he passed some of it on to the family boss. And one of the reasons John Gotti was at odds with Paul Castellano was because Gotti's crew was into the drug business in a big way selling heroin and Castellano was pissed off about it. He didn't mind collecting his envelope. But he was worried that if those guys got busted, it would be bad for the family's image.

"I'll tell you how this made-man thing really worked in New York City. In order for guys to get straightened out [become made], their names had to be submitted to the Commission [the heads of the five New York City crime families] when the books were open. Opening the books was like an enrollment period. And all the families opened the books at the same time. It didn't happen that often, because with all the pressure the law was putting on, it was tough to get the five bosses together in the same place at the same time. It might happen once a year or it could be a couple of years between enrollments.

"When the books did open, the crew boss gave his list of candidates to the head of the family, who put the names in front of the Commission. Any of the five bosses could block anybody's name regardless of what family the guy was associated with.

"Let's say the nominee had robbed somebody from another family's crew, then didn't make it up. He might have borrowed money and didn't pay it back. Or maybe he went into an establishment run by another family and acted like a cowboy, getting in fights and causing damage. Any of these things could be seen as meaning the guy wasn't honorable or mature enough to become a member. He could get a no vote because one of the five thought he was too young and needed more seasoning.

"Contrary to popular belief, money and politics play a big part in whose names get submitted and who get their badge [are inducted]. I know of people who had lots of money and bought their way in. I'm talking about guys who never broke an egg, much less shot or killed anybody. You'd be surprised at how quick tradition goes out the window when a wannabe dangles a hundred thousand dollars under a boss' nose. But these types want the prestige of being made. They don't really want to work with or run a crew. So other than making a mockery of the eligibility requirements, they don't really hurt anything.

"The same isn't true in other cases, though. I said earlier that the Mob is rife with nepotism. When a boss sponsors a blood relative or close friend for membership who isn't qualified, problems can result. I mean, how much credibility will a guy have when he orders somebody to do some work if he's never pulled the trigger himself?

"When I was doing time in a federal prison in 1997, a Lucchese capo named Georgie Conte was inside with me. He was a trigger man with a solid reputation and was highly respected. He told me about how one guy tried to get around that requirement. Another Lucchese capo wanted to get his son made, but the kid had never committed an act of violence. So the son was assigned to participate in a murder. A few days before the hit, the kid went to Georgie's home. He admitted that he couldn't go through with the murder. He wanted Georgie to do the killing for him for fifty thousand and give him the credit for it. Georgie turned him down and the kid didn't go on the hit. But his father had enough clout that he got made anyway.

"Some people aren't capable of doing violence and I'm okay with that. But don't put somebody like that in a position of power where he can order people to do what he doesn't have the guts to do himself.

"And there are lots of guys who deserve to get in, but don't. Maybe they don't kiss the boss' ass enough. Maybe they're too good at their job and pose a threat to the boss. Those capos aren't about to give more power to somebody who could end up replacing them.

"These things don't sit well with some of the old-time made men or the younger guys waiting for their chance. But what can you do about it? Even John Gotti bent the rules to get his son made. So in the modern-day Mafia, you can get your badge if you've got enough money, know the right people, or are a big enough earner.

"And the benefits of being a made man aren't cast in stone, either. It all depends on who does what to whom. For instance, Gambino crewman Roy DeMeo [car thief and cold-blooded killer] could get away with about anything he wanted to, because everybody was afraid of him. He could take out a made man and nobody said shit. If somebody not as strong looked at a made man the wrong way, he could get the death sentence.

"But in 1988 I thought there was a good chance Nicky would put my name in when the books opened. I'll never know whether he would have or not, because Ralph Burzo came along. And that deal blew me out of contention."

RALPH BURZO

As described in the first chapter of this book, on April 8, 1988, Andrew shot a man named Ralph Burzo. In order to put that incident in context, it was necessary to review several years of his life immediately prior to the shooting. That accomplished, Andrew can tell his side of the story, explaining what happened that day and in the days that followed.

"At that time my relationship with Dina was strained. We weren't living together. She was staying with her mother and I'd started dating another girl. Had she not been carrying my child, we probably wouldn't have been in contact at all. But Dina said she wanted me to be at the hospital when the baby was born and asked me to attend Lamaze classes with her. She also told me she needed a car to get to the classes and doctor appointments. So I gave her a substantial amount of cash to buy a car. She said she had an uncle who ran a car lot and she'd get something from him. A day or two later, she came to the horse room on Stillwell Avenue driving a green Thunderbird. She said she'd purchased the car from her uncle.

"That night, I went to her place to go to the Lamaze class. My new girlfriend was using my car, so we took the Thunderbird. On the way, the cops pulled us over for a traffic violation. They ran the plate and checked the insurance card and found everything had expired three years earlier. I asked her how her uncle could have let her drive out of his dealership with no insurance and expired plates. She gave me a story that I bought, but it turned out to be a lie.

"After the class we went back to her mother's and I spent the night. The next morning we went outside and as we approached the car, I saw this guy there changing the windshield wipers. I'd never seen him before and had no idea who he was. He was about ten years older than me and looked like a weight lifter. He wasn't that tall, but he was stocky—around two hundred forty pounds or so. I thought maybe he worked for Dina's uncle and he'd been sent over to put on the new blades.

"I didn't know it at the time, but I learned later that as I was getting close to the car, Dina was walking behind me gesturing to this guy to get out of there. When we got to the Thunderbird she said, 'Andrew, this is Ralph.' Ralph didn't say hello or offer to shake hands. He just turned around and walked away.

"I asked Dina who in the hell he was. Did he work for her uncle? Now the tears and the truth came. She told me that Ralph was the guy she bought the car from, not her uncle. She'd been afraid to tell me that.

"I asked her how much she paid for it. She said she hadn't actually given him any money yet. He was letting her use the car for a while. The more I heard, the less I liked the arrangement. The lies had me pissed off. And I knew deals like that usually come with strings attached.

"Dina drove me back to my house and I called my buddy

Sammy [Karkis]. I told him I had a situation that was buggin' me. I wouldn't get my own car back until later and asked him to drive me around to look for this Ralph guy, so I could get to the bottom of what was really going on. Sammy picked me up and we drove back over toward Dina's. As we drove down East Second Street, there was Ralph, walking down the block.

"I got out of the car, walked up to him, and told him we had to talk. I said we had to get the car business straightened out. Dina didn't need favors from anybody. If he wanted to sell the car, we'd buy it. That's the way it had to be.

"Ralph had a bad attitude right from the start. He said that was a matter between him and Dina and he wasn't going to talk with me about it.

"I said, 'You're telling me that what goes on between you and Dina is none of my fuckin' business? I'll tell you somethin' right now. If you want trouble, you've got the right guy. This is your lucky day.'

"Ralph wasn't impressed. He said, 'I don't give a shit who you got in that car or who in the fuck you think you are. I'll give you a beatin' and him too.'

"Now I was really pissed off. This motherfucker thinks he's going to tell me that what he does with the mother of my child is none of my business and get away with it? I didn't want to back off and I couldn't have even if I did. Here I was thinking about getting made and I'm gonna let this prick back me down? If I couldn't handle a guy trying to make a move on my woman, where in the fuck was I goin' in the family?

"Ralph started to take off his windbreaker to be ready to fight. As he did, he turned his head slightly. I pulled the thirty-eight out of my pants and shot him behind his ear. Lucky for both of us the bullet struck bone and splintered. He went down, but he was alive and conscious. I squatted next to him and was ready to fire a second round into his head to finish him off. Before I pulled the trigger, I looked around and this old woman was looking right at me. I stood up, put the gun back in my pants, and jumped in the car with Sammy. We drove past the woman and made our getaway.

"After a couple of blocks, I had Sammy pull over. I got out of the car and threw the gun on the roof of a body shop. Then he dropped me off at the horse room.

"I borrowed a car and drove around for a while. I called Nicky's future son-in-law Vinnie Dragonetti and Anthony Gerbino and told them what happened. Then I went to a friend's house, took a shower, and changed clothes. After that I returned the borrowed car and got my own car back. I called Dina, picked her up, and drove to her father's home in New Jersey. I figured I'd be safe there until I could find out if the cops were trying to find me. At that point Dina knew something was up, but I hadn't told her the whole story yet. By the time we got to her father's, the police had already been to Dina's mother's place looking for me.

"I found out later that the reason the cops got onto me so quick was because Ralph was in and out of consciousness. When he was awake, he told them he didn't know what happened to him. The last thing he remembered for sure was talking with somebody named Andrew. He didn't know my last name, but he described me as Dina's husband. He also told them that I had been in a car with a kid named Sammy. I was totally unaware that Ralph had met Sammy previously. He didn't know his last name either, though. With all that information, they figured me to be the Andrew guy pretty fast and the search was on.

"When the cops went to my mother's, they said they wanted to speak with her about her son. Right away she thought I was dead and they showed up to give her the news. They told her I was wanted for questioning in connection with a shooting—I wasn't the victim. She shut the door on them. When they drove away, she got in her car and met up with Mike Yannotti, Anthony, and Richie. They went to the street where I told Anthony I'd thrown the gun on the roof to find it and get rid of it. They rode up and down that area on the elevated subway checking the roofs and couldn't locate the gun. It was never found. Not by them and not by the cops. To this day I have no idea what happened to it; it just disappeared.

"When Dina's father found out the cops were looking for me, he didn't want me in his house. Dina and I headed back to New York. I couldn't take her right to her mother's, because the cops would probably be watching the place. I gave her some money, told her I'd be in touch, and dropped her off a few blocks away. I didn't tell her anything about where I might go or what I might do.

"From there I drove to the home of a childhood friend. He wasn't in the life and the law would never connect me with him. I let my mother know I was okay and where I was. I spent the night there and the next morning my mother called me from a pay phone. She said she'd reached out to my father and he was coming to get me and help me get away.

"I hadn't seen my father since I don't know when. He did come and get me, though, and we went to his father and mother's old house in the Williamsburg section of Brooklyn. They had both passed away, but the family still owned the place. We stayed in the basement apartment overnight, making plans and setting up the escape. The next morning we were gone."

STAYING FREE

Andrew and his father caught a plane from New York to Los Angeles. They immediately took another flight to Las Vegas, then a bus to Laughlin, Nevada. Laughlin is located on the Colorado River about 90 miles south of Las Vegas. Directly across the river from Laughlin is Bullhead City, Arizona. So three days after the Burzo shooting, the DiDonatos were in the growing tourist destination on the Colorado. But they weren't lazing around gambling or taking in the sights like tourists. They were keeping busy trying to figure a way out of his predicament.

They checked in with Andrew's mother and she said the cops had been by again looking for him. They told her if he didn't turn himself in, they'd put him on "America's Most Wanted." Andrew contacted a lawyer in New York named Ed Rappaport. This guy represented a lot of cops who had been charged with corruption or some other misconduct. He had a reputation for being able to get people off. Through him, Andrew and the cops reached an agreement that he'd surrender at the 69th Precinct on May 3. Part of the deal was that Andrew could put up bail after he was arraigned. He'd be able to stay free.

They went back to New York a few days ahead of time on April 28. Andrew went to his sister's house and arranged to have Dina come over. The excitement must have been too much for her, because within an hour of her getting there, her water broke and she was rushed to the hospital. He couldn't go with her; he was still a wanted man and the cops would have arrested him, on sight. Andrew's son was born that day. Even amidst the uproar, it was an emotional time for Andrew. He and Dina named the boy Andrew Dominick.

Andrew surrendered as promised and got out on bail the next day. His maternal grandfather put his house up as collateral for the bond. He volunteered to do it, which shocked Andrew's mother. He'd always liked his grandson, who used to take him fishing and to his doctor appointments. He knew Andrew was a gangster. He just said not to bring any trouble around to his house.

"So now I was back on the street," Andrew explains. "But I had to lie low and even give up my horse room. If I got pinched again for anything, they'd revoke my bond on the attempted-murder charge. My income dropped to almost nothing and I knew I had major legal expenses ahead of me. I was getting all kinds of advice that I should marry Dina, because a newlywed with a baby might get some sympathy from a jury. On May twenty-fifth, we tied the knot in a small ceremony.

"And my brother-in-law helped me out by lining me up with a job. He was an engineer with a company in Manhattan and he got me a job at Madison Square Garden steam cleaning the outside steps and sidewalks. The job started very early in the morning before there was much pedestrian traffic. The company I was working for wanted its employees to look professional. We were required to wear uniforms that included a bow tie.

"It was my first day. It was summertime and it was hot. On top of that I was using steam, which made it twice as hot. I had my shirt off and was in my tank top doing my thing. All of a sudden this guy walks up to me. He says, 'Excuse me. You work for such and such a company, don't you?'

"I said I did. He said he did too. He told me his name and that he was watching me from his office window across the street and noticed I wasn't in uniform. I said, 'Well, I'm using the steam cleaner and that's two hundred twenty degrees. And the temperature today is about another hundred. I don't know what you expect me to do.' He said, 'Well, I expect you to be in uniform.'

"I said, 'You were in your air-conditioned office watching me work and you decided to come down here and bust my balls because I'm not wearing a bow tie? Get the fuck outta here!' And then I started to squirt him with the steam hose. I chased him down the steps of Madison Square Garden with the steam machine. Needless to say, I got fired. That was the first legitimate job I ever had and it only lasted a few hours."

SAM KARKIS

When Sam Karkis was questioned after the Burzo shooting, he told the police they had the wrong guy. He'd been working that day. When further investigation revealed that Sam's story wasn't true, he was indicted on the same charges as Andrew, plus an obstruction count for lying to police investigators. Andrew asked his lawyer to arrange for an associate to represent Karkis.

As time passed, Andrew believed the prosecution had a very weak and beatable case. Burzo himself couldn't remember what happened to him. The closest he could come to naming Andrew as his assailant was to place him at the scene. The only witness, Mrs. Raiola, was unable to positively identify Andrew as the man she'd seen arguing with and squatting next to Burzo that day. And the gun hadn't been found.

Andrew's financial situation even got a boost when Karkis tipped him off to a drug dealer who was ripe for a robbery. Andrew made about $18,000 on the score and was able to kick some money up to Nicky, which pleased them both.

All in all, Andrew was feeling pretty optimistic about his situation—until the air started seeping out of his balloon when he learned that Karkis had switched lawyers, which is one of the early-warning signs of trouble for a person facing criminal charges. When a co-defendant changes lawyers, it's often an indication he's considering cooperating with the prosecution. And that was exactly what went through Andrew's mind when he heard that Karkis had fired his Ed Rappaport-arranged attorney.

Andrew talked over the Karkis situation with Anthony Gerbino and Mike Yannotti. After that Vinnie Dragonetti went to see Sammy at his house. He told Sammy they didn't care what lawyer he used. But then he reminded him that in his previous statements, he said he didn't remember what happened the day Burzo was shot. And that it would be in his best interests to stick with those statements come trial time.

"I could see the writing on the wall, though," Andrew says. "Sammy started avoiding me like I had the plague. I got with Anthony and Mike again to talk about what we were going to do about him. The decision was that we couldn't kill Sammy on speculation. But if he did actually become a witness, Anthony and Mike would deal with him personally.

"I'd always been there for those guys when they needed help, so I wasn't surprised by their promise. And I felt pretty good knowing that even if Sammy screwed me and I went to prison, he'd pay with his life."

● ● ●

Andrew spent the balance of the year struggling to earn enough money to pay his mounting legal fees and the added expenses related to having a wife and son to support. All the while, he was wondering whether Sammy Karkis had decided to turn against him.

That December the books were opened and several gangsters were straightened out. Among them were John Gotti's son Junior Gotti and Michael "Mikey Scars" DiLeonardo. But being made together doesn't necessarily mean you'll stay together.

11

Trial ...

For Andrew, 1989 began with financial, legal, and domestic problems that got worse as the months went by. He, Dina, and Andrew Junior were living together in an apartment on East 80th Street in Canarsie. The stress caused by his inability to earn like he had in the past and preparing for his upcoming attempted-murder trial strained his already fragile relationship with Dina. All thoughts of moving up in the Gambino family were gone, at least temporarily. Just keeping his head above water financially was a struggle.

"Those were tough times," Andrew remembers. "I couldn't work my rackets like I used to. And when I did make a few bucks, about seventy-five cents out of every dollar went toward my lawyer. I blamed Dina and her lies for putting me in the situation with Burzo to begin with.

"About the only bright spot was the weakness of the case against me. I knew if I could get a walk on those charges, I'd be back on my feet in no time. So even though it seemed like I was always in court for some kind of motion hearing and Rappaport always wanted more money, I still thought things would work out for me. And then Rappaport pulled the rug out from under me.

"We were in court for a pre-trial hearing in May and he told the judge that I wasn't living up to my financial commitment to him. He asked to be released from the case. I wanted to take the eyes right out of his head. I had paid him around forty thousand already and he hadn't done anything except go to hearings. He wanted the balance—I think it was ten or twelve thousand—or he wanted the judge to cut him loose.

"I stood there next to him whispering things like, 'I gave you all this money and now you can't take payments, you low life motherfucker?' He didn't back down, though. He wanted more money and that was that.

"The judge backed him. She said she'd give me seven days to pay up or she'd see to it that I hired another lawyer. Then she asked me if I could afford to pay for a new attorney. I said, 'How the fuck can I pay for another lawyer after I gave this motherfucker almost forty thousand?' So we had this big argument in the courtroom and, of course, I lost.

"After that, Rappaport, my father and me were out in the hallway. My father was almost as pissed off as I was. I told Rappaport I felt like knocking his teeth right out of his fuckin' mouth. We argued back and forth for a while. But when it was all over, the bottom line was that I had a week to come up with the rest of the money or else he was out. I left that courthouse boiling. I was mad at Rappaport and so frustrated about the money that I was ready to start pulling my own hair out.

"I contacted some of my drug-business associates and was able to come up with about eighty-five hundred. Now I was so close to having Rappaport's money that it was pretty much a done deal. All I had to do was see Nicky for the balance."

TOUGH LOVE

The reason Andrew thought the influx of money from his drug buddies had pretty much solved his immediate financial problem was that Nicky Corozzo, after all, was a millionaire. Andrew had shown his loyalty to Nicky many times and made a lot of money for him over the past several years. And didn't Nicky call him Good News because of the tremendous profits he'd generated through the horse room? Certainly, Nicky wouldn't hesitate to loan him four or five grand. It was a no-brainer.

"I met Nicky on the street outside our social club. I explained what was going on with Rappaport and that if I didn't pay him off, I'd lose the forty thousand I'd already paid and my best shot at getting an acquittal. Then I asked him for the loan.

"Nicky said, 'Hey, it's not about the money. I'd do anything for you, you know that. But you gotta understand. I've got thirty or forty guys coming around all the time looking for this and that. When Lenny [DiMaria] and me were coming up, Fat Andy [Anthony Ruggiano, Nicky and Lenny's crew boss] never bailed us out right away if we got pinched. He let us sit in jail a few days to see if we could get out on our own. You see, in this life, you've gotta exhaust every other avenue available to you before you ask for help.'

"Right after saying, 'It's not the money; I'd give it to you in a minute,' he asked me, 'If I give you five thousand and you end up gettin' convicted and sent away for ten or fifteen years, how would I get my money back?'

"This was a side of Nicky I'd never seen before. I stood there looking at him and I thought, you dirty motherfucker. I tried not to let him know how hurt I was. I just told him he knew better than me and I understood.

"He said he didn't want me upset, that I had to look at this from a business perspective. I told him I'd proved my loyalty over and over again. If I had to go out gun in hand to get his money back to him, I'd do it. But I wasn't going to argue with him about it. He knew best and I was okay with it.

"But it stayed with me for a long time. I think I eventually figured out why Nicky did what he did. I'd been loyal to him, but I never kissed his ass like a lot of them did. And he was pissed off about the Burzo shooting for two reasons. It wasn't business—it was personal. Because of it, I had to give up the horse room where we were making a killing. And that hurt him in the wallet.

"What he didn't consider was that the reason I shot Burzo was because I had to prove myself. What the hell good would I be to the Gambino family if I couldn't handle a problem in my own household? And how would me letting Burzo slide have reflected on Nicky and the crew? It was because of the life that I had to deal with Burzo decisively. I thought then I had no choice but to shoot him. Looking back at it now, I know better. Ralph Burzo didn't deserve what I did to him. But that's water over the dam.

"As I walked away from Nicky that day, I'd learned a couple of things. In that life, you never let anyone know what you're thinking or feeling. And it's okay to walk away and live to fight another day. But don't forget. Don't ever forget."

THE TRIAL

Andrew was unable to meet Rappaport's financial demands within the allotted seven days. When his trial started after Labor Day, he and his court-appointed lawyer shared the defense table with his co-defendant Sammy Karkis and his counsel. Andrew's father, Dina, Anthony Gerbino, Mike Yannotti, and a few more of his friends were also in the courtroom.

However, although they were still living together, by this time Andrew and Dina's marriage was damaged beyond repair. Andrew blames the deterioration in their relationship on two things: Ralph Burzo and youth.

"I found out over the summer there was a lot more to the thing between Burzo and Dina than the car. I blamed her for not letting me know earlier that he was harassing her. And during the trial I found out a lot more. He'd actually been stalking her—calling on the phone and sending candy and flowers. Her mother knew about it. Her brother knew about it. Everybody knew about it but me. I felt like a real sucker. So I had an attitude toward her and my friends hated her.

"The other thing is that we were so young. We really weren't much more than kids ourselves and there we were with a baby and all kinds of financial and legal problems. I don't think we were mature enough to handle it all.

"In the days leading up to the trial, my new lawyer had told me that the prosecution had a very weak case. They had no eyewitnesses and no gun. He couldn't understand why the case was even going to trial. According to him, the only thing I had to fear was Sammy Karkis. He said if Sammy turned, we'd have to discredit him somehow. But that would be hard to do. Any illegal activity he was involved in that I knew about I was in on too. I couldn't point the finger at him without admitting my own guilt. My lawyer was right. If Sammy went to the other side, I was in trouble.

"Something else bothered me. If the prosecution case was that weak, why hadn't they made me an offer? They sometimes made deals even when they had solid evidence just to get a quick and inexpensive conviction. But they hadn't reached out to me at all.

"And then Sammy's name showed up on the witness list. Not as a prosecution witness, but as a potential witness to testify on his own behalf. I wasn't real comfortable with that. On the opening day of the trial, though, Sammy was right there sitting at the defense table with me. I thought that maybe I was just being paranoid."

The trial started off well for Andrew. As expected, Ralph Burzo testified that his last memory on the day of the shooting was that he was talking with Andrew. But he couldn't swear that Andrew shot him. The prosecution called no witnesses who could identify Andrew as the gunman.

However, by a couple of days into the trial, Andrew was sure that his concerns about Sammy were well-founded. His co-defendant acted very uncomfortable around him. He was evasive and wouldn't make eye contact. And then Andrew and his lawyer's worst fears came true. Sammy took the stand and his testimony was far from strictly "on his own behalf." The prosecution had its eyewitness.

"As soon as Sammy started talking, it was obvious he was the prosecution's secret weapon," Andrew recalls. "Anthony Gerbino and Mike Yannotti were sitting in the back of the courtroom. Anthony started hollering out things about rats and was evicted. Mike moved up to the front row, leaned forward in his chair, and stared at Sammy. You could tell Sammy was getting the message that he was a dead man. He looked at the ceiling, the floor, and the side walls. His eyes went everywhere but forward where he'd have to see Mike and me.

"Sammy was feeling the heat, but he talked anyway. He took the jury through the events of April eighth: my call to him, seeing Burzo on the street, the shooting, ditching the gun, all of it. As I listened to him, I was upset with myself that I hadn't taken care of Sammy personally. My lawyer wrote a note on his legal pad and passed it to me. It said, 'The fat lady just sang.' I wrote, 'Go fuck yourself,' and handed the pad back to him.

"Right after Sammy finished his testimony, the judge sent the jury out of the room. She then told me that so much incriminating evidence had been presented that she now considered me to be a flight risk and revoked my bail. I motherfuckered her under my breath. She asked me what I'd said. I told her I'd asked somebody to send me a sweat suit to wear in jail. As I walked past the guard in the back of the room, he said, 'I've been watching this case since day one. You'd have beat this case without that guy [Karkis]. You know that, don't you?' Yeah, I knew it.

"During the recess my lawyer said I had two choices. I

could let things stand, get convicted, and go to jail. Or I could take the stand myself and claim the shooting was an accident. He said that with all the testimony about Burzo being a stalker, I could say that when I confronted him he pulled a gun. We wrestled around and the gun went off. It was a long shot, but it was the only chance I had.

"I thought about it. Guys in the life aren't supposed to take the stand. My situation was different; the shooting wasn't business related. Cross examination would be limited to my case and not get into anything about the crew. I wasn't excited about it. But I figured what the hell. Why not take the chance?

"I took the stand and committed perjury. I testified that Burzo had pulled a gun on me and I thought he was going to shoot me. In self-defense I tried to get the gun away from him and during the struggle it went off. The jury didn't buy my lies in the least. They returned in what must have been almost record time, probably a little less than an hour, and found me guilty on all counts. I was facing a prison sentence of five to fifteen years.

"Sammy wound up getting convicted of hindering prosecution and got sentenced to thirty days on Riker's Island. Even so, I felt good knowing he was under a death sentence from Anthony and Mike. With that thought, and a smirk on my face, I was taken away to the Brooklyn House of Detention to await sentencing."

WELCOME WAGON

Andrew's first 24 hours in the House of Detention were memorable. He found himself to be the only white man on his tier.

Just a few weeks earlier on August 23, a 16-year-old black male named Yusef Hawkins had been killed by a gang of white youths in Bensonhurst. Hawkins and three friends had gone to the area to inquire about a used car. Unfortunately for them, the gang was prowling the neighborhood looking for blacks or Hispanics who were believed to be dating white girls living there. When they saw Yusef and his friends, the whites attacked and Yusef was shot dead. Racial tensions were running high both on the streets and behind bars.

"I'd never been a prejudiced guy," Andrew explains. "I always judged men individually by their merits. But you can go into prison that way and very easily come out a racist because of what goes on inside the walls. The House of Detention was my first real taste of it.

"I was in a pretty rotten mood to begin with. I was sitting on the bunk in my cell thinking about a lot of things when the welcome wagon showed up. The black inmates on the tier were there with their greeting. They started in on me, busting my balls. They even said I looked like one of the white boys that murdered Yusef Hawkins. I told them I wasn't part of their problems and to leave me the fuck alone.

"That night I had to make a phone call to my house. For prisoners, the phone is a lifeline. They'll fight for the phone and even kill over it. I was on the phone and this black inmate told me it was his phone time and I had to hang up. I answered him that I wasn't giving up the phone. I said I'd just been convicted of a major crime and I needed five minutes on the phone to take care of some important stuff. After that, it was all his. That didn't satisfy him and we started fighting right then.

"A white guard came in and broke us up. There were thirty of us on the tier and he locked us all in our cells. I sat on my bed listening to all the chatter from the blacks. 'You're dead, white boy,' and shit like that. Somebody called me a racist motherfucker and that he was gonna get me for killing Hawkins. I said, 'I didn't kill Hawkins, but I'm gonna kill you when they open this fuckin' door.'

"The white correction officer came over to my cell and

said, 'A white guy with heart. I love that.' Then he said, 'By the way, thanks for loaning me that pen,' and he handed me a ballpoint pen. He asked me if I knew what to do with it. I said, 'Just open this cell and you'll see what I do with it.'

"About a half-hour later, they cracked open all the cells. As soon as I got outside the same black kid and I got into it again. This time when they broke us up, they took me over to another tier. I could hear the black guy hollering to his buddies over there, 'Kill that white motherfucker.'

"In the cell next to me was a Hispanic guy. He couldn't speak English and didn't have a tooth in his head. Through sign language and a word here and there that he understood, we made friends and started hanging around together. He was a barber and cut inmate's hair. I found out he was a triple murderer waiting to be sentenced. We hit it off good. He was a tough guy and he watched my back.

"Other white guys came in from time to time. But they were mostly there for drug stuff. Some of them had mental issues and would go to the psych unit and you wouldn't see them again. It was tough to develop any solid relationships with those guys, because they tended not to be around that long. Because of that I hung around mostly with the Hispanics."

At the end of September, Andrew was sentenced to five to fifteen years in state prison. He was expecting it, so it came as no surprise. He even thought it wasn't really that bad. Because of overcrowding, New York corrections tried to get inmates out as quickly as possible, so there was a good chance he'd only have to do the short end.

As Andrew accepted his situation, it didn't seem as bleak as it did on the day he was convicted. He felt serving five years wasn't the end of the world. Friends on the street would keep an eye on Dina and his son and make sure they were taken care of.

And he had the promise of Gerbino and Yannotti that

Sammy Karkis would be dealt with. He knew it would be awhile before that happened, because an immediate hit would draw a lot of suspicion and heat. But it was something to look forward to.

On October 13, Andrew was shipped out of Brooklyn to Riker's Island for one night, then on to the state prison system and a whole new world.

... and Tribulation

To the average person, the thought of the clanking noise as the steel bars of a prison gate closes behind them is terrifying. The uncertainty of what awaits him and not knowing exactly how long he'll be locked up can drive some first-time prisoners to the point of suicide.

But Andrew wasn't the average person when he entered the New York State penal system on October 13, 1989. He was a tough young man and his experiences had made him better suited to handle whatever was thrown at him behind bars than those who were less streetwise. He walked through the barred gate with a swagger in his step and the smirk still on his face.

"On the outside, I was acquainted with plenty of guys who had done time, so I had a basic understanding of what I was in for," Andrew says. "Unlike a lot of first-timers, I went into the state system knowing how quickly my back could be up against the wall. I knew that when I got inside, who I'd been on the street meant nothing. Prison inmates only respect toughness and your willingness to commit violence and inflict harm. I knew I might have to kill in order to protect myself. And I was mentally and physically prepared to do whatever I had to do to stay alive."

Andrew's first stop was at the Downstate Correctional

Facility, a maximum-security prison located in the village of Fishkill, New York, about 70 miles north of New York City. Downstate serves primarily as a classification center for new inmates entering the New York State prison system. New inmates typically remain at Downstate for a few weeks before being assigned to a permanent facility. He wasn't impressed with his temporary home.

"This place was totally designed to break the inmate from his street mentality. It reminded me of what I'd heard about military boot camps, that they play with your head. The first thing they did when I got there was delouse me. Then they shaved my head. They try to strip the new arrivals of their identity.

"After that come the interviews to gather information that will determine what facility you're assigned to next. Your criminal history and current charges are considered too. I was classified as a maximum-security inmate and told I'd be going to a place where there were other guys like me— guys prone to violence with lengthy maximum sentences. It was funny to see some of the guys I'd been in the House of Detention with, guys who had been actin' pretty tough suddenly playin' like altar boys because they were so fuckin' afraid of ending up in places like Attica, Dannemora [Clinton Correctional Facility], or Comstock [Great Meadow Correctional Facility]."

After about three weeks, Andrew was told that he was being moved to Sing Sing. Other than Alcatraz, Sing Sing is probably the most iconic prison in the United States. It's located 30 miles or so north of the Big Apple in the village of Ossining, New York, on the banks of the Hudson River and for years it was the home of New York's electric chair. Believing he'd arrived at his final destination, Andrew was somewhat concerned about what he saw shortly after arriving.

"I'd only been there a little while and was in the holding area. All of a sudden I saw this inmate coming toward me. He was a white guy with a full Santa Claus-like beard. He was wearing a dress and had fake boobs. I started laughing, thinking they'd sent me to an insane asylum."

But for better or worse, Andrew was only at Sing Sing for a few hours before his final transfer. He was placed on a bus to the Coxsackie Correctional Facility, 27 miles south of Albany. On the trip he made a friend.

"I was shackled to an Irish kid named Patty O'Keefe. We hit it off right from the start. He was tough and seemed to know his way around. He told me this wasn't his first rodeo [trip to prison] and schooled me about what would happen when we got to Coxsackie. He said that first and foremost, we had to stick together. If we did, we'd be a force to be reckoned with.

"His words proved true within our first few hours at Coxsackie. We were in a reception unit where transfers in and out of the facility were processed. We were locked down awaiting our first recreation period, which in the reception unit lasts two hours. As we waited, I overheard a black inmate who was being transferred out of the facility telling a group of new black prisoners about how to extort the white convicts. I'd gotten a taste of racism in the House of Detention, so what I heard didn't surprise me. It did piss me off, though. I knew I had to cut the problem off at the knees, just like I did in Brooklyn. If I didn't, I'd be in for a real bad time.

"No sooner did I come to that realization than I looked out the window of my cell door and saw Patty O'Keefe staring back at me from his cell across the corridor. I could see the rage on his face and knew he'd heard the same things I did. Using sign language, we motioned to each other that when the gates opened for recreation, we would attack the racist bastard. He was too fuckin' arrogant to see it coming. Somebody like him would never think a couple of new white guys would have the balls to come after him.

"When the doors opened, I got out of my cell fast and

waited for the extortionist to show his face. When he stepped from his cell, it was pretty obvious he'd been upstate for a while and spent a lot of his time lifting weights. As he walked by me to get to the rec room, Patty came from behind and tapped him on his shoulder. When he turned around Patty hit him a shot and he landed on the floor right at my feet. That's when I started putting the boots to him. Patty joined me and we hollered, 'Extort us, you motherfucker!' as we beat him unconscious. The other blacks froze, not knowing what to do as they saw their fearless leader beaten and kicked to a pulp by two white guys—the same whites they'd been told they could victimize. Now their teacher was a victim himself. A victim of his own methods.

"Seconds later, the response team rolled in, pinning me and Patty to the wall and cuffing us. I was kept locked in my cell until the next day. Then an officer came and told me I was released from lockup. Patty wasn't, though. He took all the weight for the beating. I figured he might have been pissed off about that. But when I looked across at his cell, he was standing there smiling at me. That moment cemented our friendship. At least for the time being.

"Within a day or so, I was out of reception and into general population. I hit the main yard and was immediately greeted by Joey Urgitano, whose father was a wiseguy with the Harlem crew of the Lucchese crime family. He said he'd spoken to Teddy Persico's girlfriend on the phone. She told him I was coming, so he was there to extend the olive branch. He told me I missed Teddy by a week. He was serving twenty years for a drug-related offense and had been transferred to Elmira [Correctional Facility] for disciplinary reasons. Joey was a great kid with a heart as big as any I ever saw. He was kind and had courage and we soon became the best of friends. Within days we both got permission to correspond with Teddy.

"After about a month in Coxsackie, I learned the politics

of the place—who was who, where I was welcome, and where I wasn't. Joey, another guy from our neighborhood named Phil 'Fat Philly' Stasio, and me soon became inseparable. On the weekend we had jobs in the school building working for a sergeant who was also from the neighborhood. He was related to the Randazzo family that ran a very popular restaurant in Sheepshead Bay. Almost immediately, me and the sergeant became very good friends. On my birthday in November, he brought me a cake from outside. He even let us cook pasta and other Italian dishes. This was obviously a great arrangement for us. But it caused jealousy among the other white inmates who resented us for our connection."

As Andrew got acclimated to prison life, he learned many valuable lessons about how the system worked. They included not only what he needed to do to make his life easier, but also the pitfalls he had to avoid.

EXTORTION, CORRUPTION, AND HOMOSEXUALITY

In society in general and prison in particular, the strong prey upon the weak. If an inmate is gullible or doesn't have the physical skills or lacks the will to defend himself, he becomes a target for the predators lurking all around him. He can be taken advantage of through violence or the threat of violence, or in more subtle ways. Andrew saw both methods in action.

"When I was at Coxsackie, the Hispanic inmates represented the majority, probably around fifty percent. Blacks were a bit behind, say forty percent or so. White inmates were the distinct minority at about ten percent. That disadvantage made it critical that we stuck together and let it be known there were no soft touches among us. But some inmates just weren't cut out to be in the prison environment. And they weren't just whites. They came in all colors. Those that didn't measure up were destined to become victims. That's just the way it was.

"When a new inmate arrived, he was watched closely by the other cons. They learned who he hung out with, whether he had any connections, if he was willing to stick up for himself. Then they found out if he had any money, how much was in his commissary account. If the guy had some buying power and was short on balls, he was targeted.

"One way to get to him would be to befriend him. The guy making the move would start talking with him. He'd ask, 'Where you from? Whatcha in for? How long?' All nice and friendly, just like he really gave a fuck. And then he'd get around to talking about commissary day—when it is, how much you can spend, what's good to purchase that can be used as prison money. Things like tuna, cigarettes, cookies, and coffee. After that comes the hook. He says that since you're new and won't be able to go to commissary for a few days, as your new friend he'll front you some stuff until you can shop for yourself. Here are some cookies. Here's a pack of smokes. And when you go to the store next week, you can pay me back three packs of cigarettes and two boxes of cookies. Once the mark agrees to that, the door is wide open.

"The old protection racket probably comes next. See those guys over there? They're looking to hurt you. For a carton of smokes I can protect you.

"And there's the more direct way to get the new guy's stuff. The real wild bunch will just wait for him to leave commissary and attack him on the way back to his unit. If he doesn't put up a fight, they'll rob him every time he goes to the store. Those things happen all the time in prison."

● ● ●

Andrew believes corruption is inherent in the criminal-justice system. Below he explains the reasons for his feelings.

"As far as local jails, such as the Brooklyn House of Detention before it was closed and Riker's Island, corruption was in the everyday fabric of the institution. For instance, many of the correction officers are African-American and some live in the same housing developments where a lot of the prisoners they're in charge of come from. The gangs these inmates are associated with make it pretty simple, 'We know you and we know your family. You do what we want, like bring in drugs and money or arrange sexual visits, or we'll hurt your family.' I know that some guards have actually been initiated into the gangs.

"In the state and federal facilities, the corruption runs a little different. At Sing Sing during the eighties, if you had two hundred dollars and the right connection, you could have a steak dinner and get laid. As for Coxsackie, that one sergeant was looking out for me and my friends. He gave us the best jobs and arranged special assignments, like going to the school building on Sundays, so we could cook pasta dinners. And he brought me that birthday cake from a pastry shop in my old neighborhood.

"When Nicky and Lenny were in the MDC [the federal Metropolitan Detention Center in Brooklyn], they had a guard on the payroll for five hundred a week. He brought them food and alcohol from the outside and arranged for them to have extra visits. He even looked into guys' cases to see who was cooperating against them or the crew. He was one of about ten officers ultimately arrested at the MDC after an investigation into corruption at that facility. Nicky and Lenny were put in the hole until they were transferred to a federal prison."

● ● ●

The general perception among the public is that most prison inmates are gang raped or engage in homosexual activity at some point. However, Andrew didn't find that kind of activity to be as prevalent as one might think.

"I can only tell you what I saw over the years I was incarcerated. But before I get into that, let me say this: The first rules of thumb in prison are don't gamble, don't fuck around with drugs, and don't mess with the homos. It's best for the new inmate if he knows that coming in or learns it damn quick. If he does, he'll avoid about eighty-five percent of the prison problems. And people need to understand that a lot of the homos in prison aren't the weak sissy-types you might find on the streets. They're some very dangerous individuals who will kill in a heartbeat. If the new inmate starts playing their game, he's taking a big chance.

"That said, my take on homosexuality in prison is that there are two types of homos. You have your flaming type, the kind who flaunts his sexual orientation. This is the guy who alters his prison uniform and personal appearance to be what he thinks is sexier and more appealing. He wears lipstick, has his hair in a ponytail, the whole bit. The other type is the tough guy who's doing a very long sentence. His attitude about his acts is, 'Hey, I'm just livin' in the moment. I have to get my ass any way I can, but I'm not really gay.' These guys live in denial. They figure that if they're the dominant partner in the relationship, they've kept their manhood. I find it ridiculous, but that's the way a lot of them think.

"For the most part, I've never seen the gang rapes that movies and television show so much. I'm not saying it doesn't happen. But in my years away, I noticed that most of the guys who got turned out were curious to begin with—making friends with individuals they knew from first sight were homos. A lot of very young kids who come through the system think if they can dominate a homosexual relationship, they'll prove their prowess. So they start hanging out with the homos, looking for someone they can control. But in the end, they become the victims.

"I've seen many so-called tough guys doing long stretches get hurt trying to take another tough guy's homo partner. Lifers will kill to get or keep a steady partner. Anyone who threatens those kinds of relationships is dealt with violently. I'd say that about ninety percent of the submissive partners come into the system already gay or with gay tendencies. The rest get turned out after they get inside."

JEALOUSY AND VIOLENCE

The animosity some of the other inmates felt toward Andrew and his friends over their perceived special treatment by the sergeant festered for several weeks. Tensions boiled over in early December, a time Andrew remembers vividly.

"I knew trouble was brewing when Patty O'Keefe approached me. He said our school jobs had to stop, that correction officers were the enemy and our cozy relationship with the sergeant didn't look good. And then a guy was caught trying to smuggle drugs into the facility. The apprehending officer was our sergeant friend. Almost immediately, rumors began to circulate that Fat Philly had given him the information about the drugs. In reality, that was bullshit. It was all about jealousy. Some of the other white inmates just couldn't stand the idea that me and my friends had a good deal going.

"A few days later, we were out in the yard. It was snowing that day with about six inches of snow on the ground. Patty asked Joey Urgitano to take a walk with him to talk about the drug thing. I watched them as they walked across the yard. I could tell there was a heated exchange of words and then Patty hit Joey. Joey fell to the ground and Patty jumped on top of him. I ran through the snow toward them as fast as I could and pulled Patty off Joey. Patty started swinging at me and we exchanged blows. Joey got to his feet and tried to go after Patty with an ice pick he'd had concealed in his clothes. But in the melee he wasn't able to get close enough to use it.

And then one of Patty's friends joined the fight.

"As we were scuffling, someone grabbed me from behind in a bear hug. I reached behind me, grabbed the guy's hair, and flipped him over my neck. When he hit the ground in front of me, I saw it was a goddamn correction officer. He was screaming in pain and I saw his arm was bent in two directions. Then the response team swarmed us. Me and Joey were handcuffed and taken to the prison assembly area, then to the nurse's office where we were stripped down and photographed. And then my troubles really began.

"I was taken to the bathroom and placed in one of the stalls with my hands cuffed above my head. The goon squad then went to work on me with fists and nightsticks for hurting one of their own. They beat me until I was a bloody mess and unable to stand. After what seemed like an eternity, they carried me to the Special Housing Unit, otherwise known as the Hole. When we got there, they put me down and told me I had to walk the rest of the way and carry my property that they'd taken from my cell. I was in tremendous pain and as I walked, I called the officers everything I could think of. That brought on an additional beating. Here I was after only a couple of months in the facility, facing charges for assaulting an officer and a shitload of time in Special Housing.

"At my hearing a few days later, I was sentenced to eighteen months in the Hole. Eighteen fuckin' months! I intentionally shot a guy in the goddamn head and got a short end of five years. They gave me almost a third as much for something that was an accident. It was ridiculous. I told the hearing officer what I thought of his decision, that I intended to file an appeal and that I'd win.

"Four months later it was determined that my civil rights had been violated and an order issued that I be released from the Hole immediately. They had to let me out, but they weren't real happy about it. They wanted to give me another tuning up before I left the unit. I told them that if another officer raised his hand to me, I'd arrange to have him shot after he got off work. I said if they didn't believe I had the connections to make that happen, all they had to do was read my file. After that, staff left me alone like I had the plague.

"So I got back into population and Joey wasn't charged for possession of the ice pick he tried to use on Patty. In fact, the weapon was never found that I know of. I can't prove it, but I'll always believe our buddy the sergeant made that ice pick disappear."

RESOLUTION

Upon Andrew's return to general population, he was reunited with his friends Joey Urgitano and Fat Philly. But as the euphoria of being out of the Hole wore off, Andrew realized that the root cause of the December incident was still smoldering under the surface.

That feeling was confirmed by Joey Urgitano, who told Andrew that the animosity from December was rising out of control. Any day things were going to pop between them and Patty O'Keefe's small group, who seemed to be Italian haters. So they made preparations to protect themselves and got ready for what was sure to come. It didn't take long.

"The following Sunday, we were in the school building where church services were held. As we waited for Patty's unit to arrive, Joey positioned himself on one side of the hallway and Philly was on the other. I was in the middle of the corridor. When Patty came in and saw me standing in front of him, it was on. Like a shot out of a gun, Patty came at me. Joey blindsided him and stabbed him twice with an ice pick. Then Philly—all three hundred pounds of him— came crashing down on him. The Irishman had no chance. I was just joining in when the response team was on us. Patty was rushed to the infirmary. Joey, Philly, and me were put in lockdown pending a full investigation. Within two days of the incident, Joey was transferred to Elmira and Philly was sent to the maximum-security Southport Correctional Facility. Mysteriously, again Joey's ice pick was never found. I stayed at Coxsackie in lockdown. Patty stayed in the infirmary for two or three days and was released back into population.

"The night-shift watch commander tried to get me to cooperate by providing information against Joey and Philly. I told him to go fuck himself with his false promises. I said he didn't even have the juice to get himself off the night shift, much less make deals for anybody else. They were unable to find a weapon or anybody to talk, so when the investigation was over, nobody got charged. Not me, not Joey, and not Philly.

"Because I wasn't charged in this case and my previous guilty finding had been reversed, I was automatically eligible for assignment to a medium-security prison. About two days after getting out of lockdown, I was transferred to the Hudson Correctional Facility. I never saw or heard of Patty O'Keefe again."

HUDSON

The improvement in Andrew's life after his transfer to Hudson Correctional Facility was dramatic. If a man had to do time in a state prison, he was convinced this was the place to do it.

He realized almost immediately he was actually going to like the place. He was there only a few minutes before he was greeted by some friends he'd made in Coxsackie. After that, he was amazed how much more freedom the inmates had. Within a year he was made secretary of the inmate Italian-American organization. They held fundraisers and he used the money to have festivals during the summer. Each member of the organization could invite his family to attend. Everybody ate together, took photos, and listened to music.

"I was with a tremendous bunch of guys in Hudson," Andrew recalls. "One of them was a capo in the Genovese family named Danny Pagano. We hit it off really well. He was a gentleman and an all-around great guy. My family and Danny's sent us hundred-pound packages of food once a month. That was enough for us and our little clique to have nice dinners every night.

"Another one of the guys from Coxsackie named Joey Jacona became a great friend of mine. Once in a while Joey and a few of the other guys would make homemade wine for all of us. We had a lot of fun. It was still prison, but all things considered, it wasn't that bad."

● ● ●

Andrew's life behind bars was tolerable overall and sometimes even enjoyable. However, as the months passed and he got closer to eligibility for work release and then parole, he experienced some disappointments. He also had to start thinking about his other life, as an associate of the Gambino family and a member of Nicky Corozzo's crew. It was a life he'd be rejoining at some point and all was far from rosy on that front.

In 1992, Andrew became eligible for work release, but he was denied because of the violent nature of his crime. It was frustrating to watch everyone around him getting into the program or out on parole. Also, by this point his relationship with Dina was distant at best. She hadn't been to see him in months and he'd stopped calling her at all.

In fact, around that time a couple of crew members came to visit and give him some advice. They said he needed to get a divorce the minute he got out of prison. It was their way of telling Andrew his wife was being unfaithful. Then word got back to him that Nicky had seen Dina outside Gambino capo

John "Jackie the Nose" D'Amico's social club. When he asked her what she was doing there, she turned white as a sheet and made up a story that she was waiting for a friend.

"I didn't really care about Dina anymore. My only concern was for my son. But I was livid about Nicky and Jackie getting involved in my personal life. And I felt the crew had betrayed me too. It seemed that when there was bad news from the street that my wife was fuckin' around on me, they couldn't get there fast enough to tell me. But what about the promise they made to me about Sammy Karkis? It was going on three years and he was still alive.

"I sent a letter out with one of my visitors for Mike Yannotti. In it I expressed my anger that after all we'd been through together, they hadn't fulfilled the promise they made to me before I was incarcerated. That letter apparently pissed Mike off. We didn't communicate for the whole year and I didn't speak to anybody else from the crew either. The only people I kept up with were my few friends from other crime families, such as Robert Arena, Teddy Persico, and Joey Urgitano. We wrote to each other once a week. As far as I was concerned, I wouldn't ask Nicky or the crew for anything ever again."

● ● ●

While Andrew was in prison, two other things occurred that later impacted his life in major ways. First, gangland strife broke out in 1991 in what became known as the Colombo War. Second, on June 19, 1992, Guardian Angel founder Curtis Sliwa was shot in the back seat of a taxi while on the way to do his early-morning radio talk show at WABC-AM. According to a *New York Times* article the following day, Sliwa was the victim of a well-planned attack.

The taxi in which the shooting occurred had been stolen two days earlier. As Sliwa settled into the back seat, a gunman who had been hiding in the front seat next to the driver sat up and opened fire. Shot several times, Sliwa tumbled out of the vehicle as it lurched around the corner at East 7th Street and Avenue B. He was rushed to the hospital and emerged from five hours of surgery in critical but stable condition.

The police had no immediate suspects and said Sliwa routinely received threats due to Guardian Angel activities and the sometimes-controversial opinions he voiced on his radio show. But speculation among those in the know was that the attempted hit was a direct result of Sliwa's radio rants against recently convicted Gambino boss John Gotti.

Even though Andrew was incarcerated at the time of the incident, he would eventually be drawn into the Sliwa shooting.

In September 1993, Andrew received some unexpected good news from the state. He'd been approved for the work-release program and would be leaving the prison in 48 hours. His next stop was the Edgecombe Correctional Facility in New York City, his residence while in the program. If all went well, he'd be released on parole a year later.

13

Back on the Street

While Andrew was in prison, a changing of the guard in the Gambino crime family took place. In 1992 the feds at long last convicted John Gotti; the former Teflon Don was sentenced to life in prison without parole. However, even though he was incarcerated, protocol called for Gotti to maintain his status as the boss until all of his appeals were exhausted. In his absence, the day-to-day operations of the family were handled by a committee consisting of Junior Gotti, Jackie "the Nose" D'Amico, Nicky Corozzo, and Andrew's old friend and Nicky Corozzo's co-boss Lenny DiMaria, who had been released from prison and officially promoted to capo. So as he left Hudson Correctional, Andrew was heading back to a slightly different landscape.

His new home, Edgecombe Correctional, was located at 611 Edgecombe Avenue, Manhattan, a multi-floor minimum-security facility used for inmates participating in the work-release program. The convicts were required to sleep on site two nights per week, in a dormitory setting rather than in cells. On those days they were subjected to mandatory drug testing. Andrew's sleep-in nights were Monday and Tuesday. He had to be in the facility by seven o'clock on those evenings. On Tuesday and Wednesday mornings he was released at 4:45 a.m. to go to work at his job as an aircraft cleaner at JFK Airport. From Wednesday through Sunday nights he was to stay at his mother's house. Violating these or any of the other rules was grounds for disciplinary action, including return to full incarceration.

However, unknown to the authorities, the man who ran the aircraft-cleaning business where Andrew was to be employed was a friend of his and a Lucchese associate. In reality, Andrew was employed there only on paper. And sleeping at his mother's five nights a week didn't last very long. He quickly made other arrangements the powers that be knew nothing about. With these freedoms, Andrew was ready to get back into business.

"When I got to Edgecombe in late September, I met with a counselor," Andrew recalls. "He called my mother to confirm my living arrangements. Then he called my friend at the airport to verify my employment. After that, I called Dina to let her know that I wanted to see my son the next morning. After the gates opened, my first stop would be at her mother's place where they were living.

"News of my release must have gone around the neighborhood like a shot. The next morning I stepped out onto the streets for the first time in four years. Parked right out in front was an Oldsmobile Regency with its motor running. As I neared the car, the window rolled down. To my surprise, Mike Yannotti was inside. Our relationship had turned pretty sour, but that morning it was all hugs, kisses, and smiles. It was as though our last year of not speaking had never happened.

"Mike told me Dina had called him and that he wanted to be the first to welcome me home. I'd barely sat down in the car than he put two thousand dollars in my hand. Then he filled me in on what had been happening with the crew. After that he talked about Sammy Karkis. Mike assured me that he'd sat on Sammy's house for a week waiting for an opening to put two [bullets] in his head. But before the right opportunity arose, Nicky sent word to back off. Before I could ask why Nicky called off the hit, he changed the subject. He said a few of the crew members were concerned that I was mad at them. They didn't want that; they just wanted things to be the way they used to be. But they were so concerned about what I might do that they went to Nicky and asked him to intervene just in case I had bad intentions. Mike told me I should see Nicky as soon as possible.

"Mike then took me over to Dina's mother's place. Everybody looked at me like they couldn't believe I was really back. I got my son out of bed and hugged and kissed him. He wasn't fully awake, but he hugged me back and it felt good. After a few minutes, I had to leave for my job and Mike gave me a ride to the airport.

"The very next day I was called to see Nicky at his social club. Instead of saying welcome home, he said, 'Everybody here loves you. These guys would do anything for ya'. If you're gonna be mad at anyone, be mad at me. I put a stop to the Karkis thing and I'll tell ya why.'

"Then Nicky explained that with all that was going on [with the Colombo war], he didn't need the heat the Karkis killing would have brought on the crew. But the hypocrite bastard was lying to me. Mike Yannotti had already told me that our crew had done work [murdered people] during the war to make it look like a retaliation hit from the other side. With the Colombos getting blamed for the killings, the Gambinos were able to keep their hands clean.

"After that bullshit, Nicky gave me this fuckin' lecture about the family. He said it was bigger and more important than him or me as individuals. We needed to do what was right for the family, and at the time it was best not to kill Sammy. And then he looked me in the eye and said, 'But now that you're home, we won't let you walk around with egg on your face. Now we'll take action and put this kid to sleep.'

"My answer was easy. I said, 'Nicky I love you and I'd

do anything for you. But I needed you when my hands were cuffed. No disrespect, but I can do this all by myself now. I've dreamed of doing it for the past four years.' With that I walked out the door. And from that day on, our relationship was never the same."

Andrew's disenchantment with Nicky prior to going to prison was growing. Not only had his boss denied him when he was in need of money before his trial, he was now lying to him to cover for his lack of loyalty.

"Look at it from my perspective," Andrew continues. "This guy was my leader. I just got home and he didn't even put a hundred-dollar bill in my pocket to help me get off and running. But friends of ours from other crime families showed a lot more class than Nicky. Wild Bill Cutolo and his son Billy Junior of the Colombos gave me a thousand-dollar welcome-home gift. Danny Pagano from the Genovese family sent me a thousand for pocket money. But not Nicky. He didn't come up with a goddamn dime. The only guy from my own crew to help me out financially was Mike Yannotti. And I didn't know if he did that out of guilt for us not speaking all those months or because of the Karkis thing. In spite of our differences recently, Mike and I always had mutual respect over the years. I decided I didn't have time to dwell on what his motivation was. I had to start earning."

It didn't take Andrew very long to get back in harness. A friend he'd made at Hudson Correctional named Mike Bolino had also made it into the work-release program and was assigned to Edgecombe. The two men quickly found something to help them make some money and pass their time: watches.

"Work release was like a breeding ground for criminals in some respects. On our sleep-in nights, a lot of the guys sat around and planned crimes. My buddy Mike was from the Court Street area in downtown Brooklyn and was affiliated with the Colombos. We wound up on the same floor at

Edgecombe and right away started working together. Mike had a connection with a guy who had access to very expensive Chaumet watches from France. I must have sold eight or ten of them my first week home. As I remember, the average price was around fifteen hundred. This was just the head start I needed. With the cash I made from the watches, I bought a few pounds of marijuana from a very good friend of mine. I gave the weed to Mike to sell and we split the profit."

Besides selling the stolen watches and marijuana, Andrew found a supplier of men's sweat suits, sneakers, and even some designer clothes to add to his inventory of hot merchandise. These sales took the financial pressure off Andrew and he needed those sources of income. Even though he was getting paychecks from the cleaning company, he was unable to access that money for a couple of reasons. First, the rules of work release prohibited the worker from cashing his check. The checks had to be surrendered to a parole officer and were held until the inmate was paroled. Second, since Andrew didn't actually perform any work at the airport, his checks were primarily loans used to create a paper trail of employment and the money had to be paid back. Andrew's arrangement was that when he was paroled and received the checks, he would cash them and then give the money, plus any withholdings for taxes, to his friend at the cleaning company.

In addition to the job scam, Andrew also violated the work-program rules by secretly taking up residence in a friend's apartment rather than staying at his mother's. This gave him a relatively safe place to stash money, marijuana, or contraband without exposing his mother to legal problems.

As the days went by and Andrew's earnings increased, he had to show up every so often to see the crew and pay his tribute to Nicky. Other than that, he spent most of his time with Billy Cutolo Junior, a man Andrew came to like very much.

"Billy was a great guy and Wild Bill, his father, was a highly respected man with the Colombos. In fact, he was one of their biggest earners. Billy and I hit the nightclub circuit together. Eventually, I started spending every Wednesday night at his father's social club with his whole crew. It was the same kind of thing my crew did on Tuesdays and Saturdays. During those Wednesday-night dinners, I got to meet a lot of new guys I became friends with. I even did business with some of them from time to time.

"My friendship with Billy was heaven sent in some ways. It allowed me to make money independently. And because Billy was a generous guy, I didn't need Nicky's help in situations where I might want to get involved in a business deal that required a large amount of capital. I even started to loan money out with Billy as my silent partner."

It didn't take long for word of Andrew's close association with the Cutolos and their crew to reach Nicky Corozzo. The wayward crew member was summoned to meet with his boss and straighten out a few things.

"In late November Nicky called me in," Andrew recalls the incident. "When I saw him, he wanted me to tell him everything I was involved in. After we discussed my many new ventures and who I was associating with, Nicky gave me a little speech. It went something like this, 'I'm glad you're home and seem to be gettin' on your feet. And I appreciate the money you been sending my way. But if you need help in any of your future ventures, your flag is here. You come to me and I'll give you what you need. As for Billy, he should know better than to try to steal you from us. You be careful, because the war over there is still lingering. He's just using you to have more shooters around him. Now listen close. I don't give a fuck who you sleep with or who you earn with. Just as long as at the end of the day when the sun sets, you come back to Sorrento [home to the crew]. You got it?'

"I smiled and said, 'One hundred percent, Nick. I was just

trying to build a little something for myself.' We embraced and I walked away. When my back was to him, a big grin crossed my face. I remember thinking, this motherfucker wouldn't give me a dime when I got released and now that I'm earning with Billy, he wants to help? And I still hadn't forgotten about that loan he denied me when I needed money for my lawyer. Fuck Nicky Corozzo! I'd still kick some of my earn to him, but I was going to hold back more for myself."

As Christmas 1993 neared, Andrew was doing pretty well financially, but his personal life was a shambles. He thought he might be able to rekindle his relationship with Dina and he gave her a Chaumet watch worth twenty-five hundred. They dated a few times, but the writing was on the wall and divorce was in the air. That was their last Christmas as husband and wife.

• • •

For Andrew, 1994 began on an up-and-down note. Although he was technically still doing time, work release was more of an inconvenience than a deterrent to his criminal activities and his earnings were on the rise. But while his social and business relationships with the Cutolos were bearing fruit, they were also further alienating him from Nicky Corozzo and his crew. Of course, there was also the unpleasant matter of his divorce from Dina.

In spite of those issues, Andrew preferred to look at the glass as being half-full.

"I started the year with optimism that I was headed in the right direction as far as my street life was concerned. As for my home life, that was a different story. Dina and I had grown apart to the point that divorce was the only option. It was unfortunate, but that's the way shit happens sometimes.

"I wasn't the only one with a headache, though. Billy Cutolo faced a crisis of his own. His father and several mem-

bers of his crew were arrested for racketeering and held without bail in the federal Metropolitan Correction Center. This
placed a lot of the responsibility for the crew's day-to-day
activities on Billy's shoulders. He wanted very much to prove
to his father and others that he was capable of handling
things and could be a good earner, but that placed him under
a lot of pressure. For the most part, Billy did a good job in his
new role.

"Under the circumstances, I tried to help Billy out as
much as I could. But the work program prevented me from
giving him all the time he needed. Parole officers stopped at
the airport every so often to verify that I was at work. The
beauty of it was that my work was in a secure area and they
couldn't just pop in unannounced. They were stopped at the
gate until my boss cleared them to come in. Sometimes I'd
be hangin' around the office playin' cards, so everything was
okay. But if I was out taking care of business, the boss had to
beep me to come in. I'd get my ass there as fast as I could and
tell the parole officer I'd been working in hangar so-and-so
and came back to the office as soon as possible. That story
always worked, but I had to stay within a reasonable distance
of the airport to pull it off.

"Finally, Billy got permission from his father to hire me
at the Gregory Hotel on Fourth Avenue in Brooklyn, which
Wild Bill owned. This was a real score for me. I think I was
gettin' six hundred a week and all I did every day was sit in
Billy's office with him and brainstorm ways for the two of us
to earn. Within a few months, we developed a healthy shylock book by loaning money to guys I knew. We also made a
few dollars selling marijuana with another member of Billy's
crew. But above all, Billy's idea of the quick buck was to bet
on sporting events. I've gotta give it to him: He was a ballsy
gambler. He'd bet four or five games a night, sometimes at
five thousand a game.

"During that summer, all the time I was spending with

Billy, bouncing around the city, and going to mob-related meetings got me some unwanted law-enforcement attention. It started when a kid close to Billy's father was subpoenaed to a grand-jury hearing. After the hearing, he came back and told Billy and me the FBI had all these photos of us. They wanted to know who I was and my relationship to Billy and the Colombo family. This is what I loved about the FBI in New York City. They never shared the information they had with other agents. If they'd shown my pictures to the other organized-crime units, the Gambino agents would have identified me. But they didn't. It took months for them to get my name when they could have had it in minutes.

"It just so happened that at that same time, I was dating a stenographer in the federal courts in Brooklyn. I mentioned the hearing and my photos to her. When she went pale, I knew she'd worked that particular hearing. Oh, how I tried to get her to give me the inside scoop. But she was a company woman and wouldn't budge. She was a great girl and I liked her very much. I didn't want to get her into any trouble, so I backed off.

"A couple of weeks later, a Lebanese guy, one of Billy's shylock customers, came into the Gregory while Billy and I were having lunch. The guy was looking to get out from under his loan and wanted to do a trade. He said he was in possession of two hundred thousand dollars worth of counterfeit hundred-dollar bills. He offered to give Billy several thousand dollars of them for free. And he'd sell him the rest cheap; I think he wanted twenty dollars each. In a matter of days we had our hands on the whole lot.

"I immediately called my friend Robert Arena and his partner and asked if they'd be interested in buying thousands of the counterfeits at a time. A few hours later they were at my apartment and our first sale was made.

"To celebrate, we took a few thousand dollars of the bogus money and went out to a sports bar. The first round of drinks came to thirty dollars or so and I paid with a fake hundred. Now we had a new earn. We'd go from club to club buyin' drinks and breakin' the bills. I took ten thousand in phony money and turned it into a full-time job to cash as many bills as possible each day. We made a killing.

"These bills were top-quality counterfeits. They were so good that when Billy got in debt to a bookie for fifteen grand on bad baseball bets, he paid the guy off with three thousand of real money and the other twelve in counterfeit. It took months for the guy to find out and make a beef.

"I was still kicking money up to Nicky once in a while and I gave him a little from the money scam. But he was still pissed off about all the time I was spending with Billy.

"It came to a head one day when I went to see him about a new business I was thinking about getting into. I knew I was in trouble when I got to the club and one of the guys gave me a warning. He said, 'When you talk with that guy [Nicky], no matter what he says, agree with him. If he tells you the walls are purple and the sky is maroon, you say okay. Understand?' I understood. I was on thin ice and if I argued with Nicky, I might not leave the club alive.

"When I saw Nicky, he said, 'So I hear you wanna be released from the crew.' Remembering the warning I'd been given, I told him I'd thought about it, but hoped we could work things out. And then he let me have it with both barrels. He said, 'If I liked you, I'd entertain the idea of your release. But I don't, so you have only one alternative. You were born here and you'll die here. And from now on, start bringing guys in the crew with you when you earn.'

"I knew at that moment my crewmate had given me good advice. If I didn't agree, my life would have been taken from me that day. So I assured Nicky there was no problem. I'd do whatever he asked. As I said those things, I knew my road with Nicky from then on would be hard and dangerous. The chances of him ever pushing to get me straightened out [be-

Andrew DiDonato—Photo with sisters
Doreen & Denise, Lorimer Street, Brooklyn (1969)

Above: Andrew DiDonato's first birthday as a free man after four years of incarceration (2001).

Below: Photo of Andrew DiDonato taken September 1996, one month after the Manalapan, New Jersey, bank robbery ($400,000). Andrew committed this crime while a fugitive from justice.

Above: Photo of
Andrew DiDonato taken
on Easter Sunday 2009.

Above Right:
New York state mug
shot of Andrew.

Right and Below:
Recent photos of
Andrew DiDonato.

Above: Billy Cutolo Jr.—Childhood friend and Colombo crime-family associate.

Right: Billy "Wild Bill" Cutolo, Sr., Colombo-family underboss. He and Andrew had their differences, but Andrew also had a deep respect for him. He disappeared in 1999 and was found dead eight years later.

Above: Danny Cutaia—Lucchese-family capo and boss of Andrew's murdered friend Robert Arena.

Below: Joe Miraglia—Genovese-family associate and a bank-robbery associate of Andrew DiDonato's.

Above: John Gotti, Jr., in 1996. Andrew's crew planned to kill John Jr., but most of them were arrested before the hit could be carried out. Andrew testified at his trial in 2005.

Right: Lenny DiMaria, on the right, one of Andrew's crew leaders within the Gambino family. He was elevated to captain status in the late '90s. Andrew had a deep respect for Lenny.

Above: Mike Yannotti was a fellow crew member of Andrew's under the leadership of Nicky Corozzo and Lenny DiMaria. In 2005, Andrew testified at Yannotti's trial, where he received a 20-year sentence.

Right:
John Gotti, Sr., Gambino-family boss from 1985 until 1991. He died in prison in 2002.

Left: Photo of Nicky Corozzo taken upon his arrest in 2008, after being a fugitive for four months. His case was featured on "America's Most Wanted!" Andrew was a member of his crew from 1983 to 1997. He pleaded guilty to murdering Andrew's two friends Robert Arena and Thomas Miranga. He will be in prison through the mid-2020s.

Below: Paul Mazzarese, a Bonanno-crime family associate and a fellow bank robber.

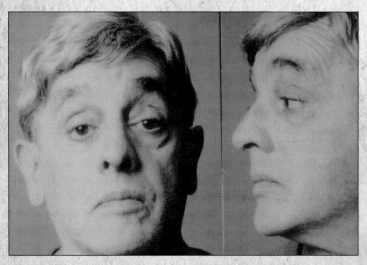

Prison photo taken of Andrew DiDonato in 1992
while doing time for attempted murder.

Above: Another 1992 prison photo of Andrew in the center, along with his father (left) and his Uncle Carmine on the right. The guys on the ends are Gambino-crew associates Mike Yannotti and Sal (Sally Lip) Bracci.

Below: Sal Demeo, a Genovese-family member and another of Andrew's bank-robbery crew. This photo was circulated when Sal went on the run for the 1996 robbery. He was the second case Andrew was involved in that had FBI most-wanted attention.

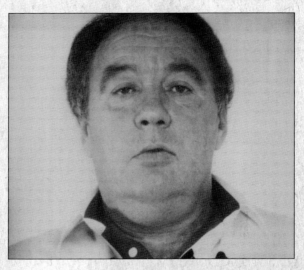

Above: Tommy Barrett, a Genovese-family associate and bank robber. While Andrew was incarcerated in federal prison, he and Tommy were in the same unit where they hatched a plan to rob a Brinks truck.

Below: Tommy Scuderi, another Genovese-family associate, the upfront man with Andrew in the New Jersey bank robbery.

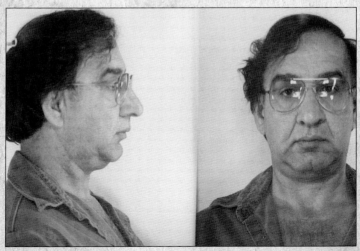

Photo of Andrew's Uncle Pasquale "Paddy Mac" Macchiarole, a capo in the Genovese-crime family, with Vincent DiDonato the day of his confirmation.

Below: 2001 photo of Andrew with his father Vincent.

come made] were remote, no matter how much I deserved it. I'd be overlooked until he taught me a lesson. And then if I started to kiss his ass like some of the other guys, maybe he'd have a change of heart. I made up my mind that he'd have to wait until hell froze over for that. I walked out of that meeting on my own power. But I knew it could easily have gone the other way."

● ● ●

As July approached, Andrew was getting ready for what was to be his first official parole hearing. In the eyes of the system, he'd accomplished 10 months of steady employment without incident. He hadn't been in trouble with the law or had any other difficulties that might hinder his chances for parole. Even the matter of his picture being shown at the grand jury was still a non-issue due to the slow identification process. The only thing Andrew had against him was the severity of his crime.

Even with all that going for him, he was extremely apprehensive. He committed so many crimes while on the work program that he walked into the hearing room expecting a shoe to drop. Just the night before, he was involved in a major drug deal with some Gambino associates from the 17th Avenue faction.

"To my total surprise, I was out of the hearing in minutes. I was told I showed a positive change and looked like I was on the road to rehabilitation, and they gave me a release date for early September. At that point I was walking on air."

Andrew had every right to be happy. His work-release jobs had been scams. He'd violated almost every program rule and resumed his life of crime as soon as he got outside of Edgecombe's gate for the first time. He was walking a fine line with Nicky Corozzo. But he'd gotten away with it all.

Free Again

Andrew was still walking on air when he attended his first official parole meeting a day after being released. He entered the office anticipating that he'd meet his parole officer, who would give him the rules and send him on his way. He had another thing coming.

He walked in, asked for his newly appointed parole officer, and was taken to his office where FBI agents and NYPD detectives immediately put him in handcuffs and told him his house was being searched. Somebody had called parole and told them Andrew was running drug and counterfeit-money rings. They had photos of him with known gangsters, probably the same surveillance images they had at the grand jury. But now they'd had identified him.

Then the parole officer said that if they found any evidence at Andrew's mother's house, they'd hit him with new charges, plus a parole violation.

"I couldn't fuckin' believe it. My first parole meeting and I was already in cuffs. And after the search was done, I knew they'd lock me up and throw away the key.

"Then I realized something. They were searching my mother's house. Whoever had dropped the dime on me must not have known about the other apartment, filled to the rafters with a new load of pot and the rest of the counterfeit money. But there was nothing illegal at my mother's. They weren't goin' to find a goddamn thing. I'm pretty sure a smile crossed my face when it hit me that I was home free.

"About five hours later, the search came up clean. The parole officer was on fire, he was so mad. What he undoubtedly thought was going to be a big feather in his cap had turned out to be nothing. His supervisor walked in and said that since they couldn't violate me, the most they could do to bust my balls was put me on a curfew. That meant I had to be at my mother's—really at my mother's—from seven at night until seven in the morning. My social life would go down to zero and business would suffer. But at least I wouldn't be locked up. Billy Cutolo got me a parole lawyer to fight the curfew on the grounds that it was harassment. After about a month, it was lifted on the condition I transfer out of Brooklyn."

Through exceptional good fortune and the help of Billy Cutolo, Andrew had managed to survive his first altercation with the parole people relatively unscathed. However, his friend Billy was in hot water of his own.

For the past nine months, Billy had been delivering payments to a number of lawyers to cover the legal fees for Wild Bill and all of his father's incarcerated crew members. On this particular day, Billy was in a panic; he didn't have all the money he needed to pay the lawyers. Andrew was a little surprised. It was common knowledge that Wild Bill was worth a fortune.

What Andrew didn't know was that when Wild Bill was incarcerated, he gave Billy access to a certain amount of money to cover legal expenses. What happened to that money? Andrew refuses to speculate about it. Whatever the reason, Billy ended up short. He knew that if the lawyers didn't get paid, his father would find out about it immediately and wonder about the rest of the money. So Billy stalled for a few days to put together the necessary cash. The pressure was on and he called in all outstanding debts.

"I owed about fifteen thousand myself for money I'd borrowed for my shylocking business. When I tried to collect the principal from one or two of the bigger loans I had out, my customers couldn't do it. One of them was my friend Mike Bolino. He was already backed up a few weeks and had just gotten pinched on top of it. This put a strain on the relationship between Billy and me, but we still worked together to try to find a solution to his problem.

"At this time I was dealing a lot of marijuana with Robert Arena from the Lucchese crew. But I wasn't making anywhere near the money Billy needed to get out from under those lawyers. What I did do was front him about twenty pounds of pot that he could sell himself on the street. I thought that with Billy's connections to some major pot movers, it could have been a great opportunity for a steady earn for him. But Billy never made a payment for the pot. I knew I owed him a lot, so I let it go. Besides, Robert and me had started moving some big numbers and shaking down drug dealers as well. So some pretty good money was now coming in. I'd still see Billy and have dinners and hang out, but the money situation had consumed him.

"In December, Wild Bill's trial was underway. I went to court a few times with Billy to show support for his dad. About a week before Christmas, Wild Bill and his crew were acquitted. I went to the party they threw at Wild Bill's social club. After having been away myself, I knew the pure joy they were experiencing just to be free. But that mood wore off quickly when Wild Bill started to inquire about how his money had been spent while he was locked up. That led to some dark days for Billy and a shitload of trouble for me too."

Starting in 1995, Andrew's life began a roller-coaster ride that made the previous years seem tame by comparison. The first week of January was an indication of a bumpy year. It began on a down note when he was summoned to a business meeting at Wild Bill Cutolo's social club. The just-out-of-jail gangster was trying to find out what had happened to the money he'd entrusted to his son while he was behind bars. And he thought Andrew knew where at least some of it had gone.

"Wild Bill said that according to Billy's records, I owed twenty-five thousand and he wanted to know when I was going to pay it back. I told him in no uncertain terms that the amount was actually about fifteen thousand and it was money that Billy and I put out on the street. He didn't like that. He said, 'You're tellin' me my son's a shylock? Billy's no loanshark.'

"I think what happened is that Billy had gone through that money somehow and did a little creative accounting to cover it up. So if somebody owed ten thousand, Billy put it down as twenty. Regardless, I didn't like Wild Bill's attitude. I told him, 'You called me in here to discuss this money and now you're treating me like a fuckin' mutt? Like I can't be trusted? Do you wanna hear the truth or don't ya? Because if you think I took that money to go sit on a beach with my wife, you're out of your mind.'

"Billy still owed Robert Arena and me fifteen thousand or so for the marijuana we fronted him. I never pushed for it and I didn't want to tell Wild Bill about it. I figured it was up to Billy to explain to his father that he'd gotten into the drug business.

"Our talk wasn't gettin' anywhere. Wild Bill said as far as he was concerned, I owed him twenty-five thousand. I told him he couldn't get twenty-five. The amount was fifteen and Billy was involved in the loans whether he wanted to hear it or not. After that I left and went on my way."

Meanwhile, Andrew was still waiting for final approval transferring his parole from Brooklyn to Staten Island.

"I was dating a girl whose father was associated with the Genovese family. He was a street guy like me and I really liked him. She got me an apartment in Staten Island and I was waiting for the parole people to okay the move.

"It was kinda funny, because Robert Arena and me had the same parole officer in Brooklyn. Sometimes I was at Robert's house counting the pounds of pot or something when this guy showed up. We weren't supposed to associate, so Robert stashed the pot while I jumped out the back window and hid in the shed.

"This particular parole officer was real strict with us. In the parole office, most of the guys waiting to see him would sit around the waiting room shooting the breeze and he didn't say shit to them. But if he saw Robert and me talking, he'd tell us to shut up or he'd violate us.

"Thankfully, my transfer to Staten Island got approved and I was able to get away from that prick. The trouble was that I lost my job at the Gregory Hotel when my relationship with Wild Bill went sour. And the parole people wanted me to show that I had a means of earning an income. I told them that I was going to be self-employed and was opening a carpet-cleaning company. I called it Andrew's Clean Machine. One of the guys I'd used the previous year to help me pass the counterfeit money gave me two floor cleaners. I'd never cleaned a carpet in my life and had no intention of doing so, but it allowed me to stay on the streets and gave me a way to account for my money. I made up phony receipts and took them to my parole officer every week. They showed I was making enough to pay my bills and put a few dollars in the bank. It worked perfect with no questions asked."

SAN DIEGO CONNECTION

With the parole matter resolved, Andrew turned his attention to a personal matter. A problem with one of his sisters' husbands had developed while he was in prison: He was not only verbally abusive, he put his hands on her. Andrew confronted him and told him he had two choices. He could act like a man and do what he was supposed to do or Andrew would put him in the trunk of a car. The choice was his.

"He gave me the excuse that he'd been in a bad way when the abuse took place. He'd gotten into drugs and wasn't himself. I told him my concern was the well-being of my sister and her children. If he could straighten up, fine. If not, he should do himself a favor and take a walk.

"He was pretty nervous and wanted to get on my good side. He said he was doing business with these two guys from an air-conditioning and refrigeration company on Utica Avenue in Brooklyn—my old stomping grounds. Maybe if I met them, we could do some things together. I said sure.

"My brother-in-law introduced me to his friends and we got along right from the start. The best thing about it was that the brother of one of them in San Diego was one of the biggest marijuana suppliers in the United States at the time. And the brother was sending marijuana to the air-conditioner place through UPS.

"Robert Arena and me made a deal for twenty pounds at a time. We wanted more, but that's all they let us have at one time until they saw how things worked out. So we got our deliveries of twenty pounds every ten days or so. Robert and I had our own distributors, including a guy who lived in a college town upstate. We funneled five pounds of weed to him out of every delivery. It was a nice marriage and we did really good with that. Our supply allotment went up to fifty pounds at a time and we were earning big time."

Andrew knew it was likely Nicky Corozzo would learn of his marijuana operation at some point. To protect himself, he slipped Corozzo some money from time to time. But he didn't pay what he should have. He held back for two reasons. One was that it galled him to pay his boss anything at all. The other was that a larger tribute would indicate the amount of money he was making. And if a guy like Corozzo knew the true amount involved, he might try to take over the operation.

His California connection was a reliable supplier for almost the entire year. However, the operation came to a halt when the guy overdosed and lapsed into a coma. As far as Andrew knows, he never regained consciousness.

In addition, his new business associates at the air-conditioning company provided him with yet another illegal earning opportunity. One of the guys had a girlfriend who worked in the main business office of Marriott Hotels. Her position there gave her access to blank checks. When Andrew heard that, he got a brainstorm. Why not get some of those checks and use them to pay Andrew's Clean Machine for cleaning carpets at the Marriott?

"The girlfriend stole an initial supply of about fifteen blank checks. Marriott's procedure was that each check had to be signed by three of its people. So each week I'd fill in one of the blank checks for ninety-five hundred dollars. We figured by keeping the amount under ten thousand, there would be less chance of the transaction getting flagged. My brother-in-law and the air-conditioner guys each forged one of the authorizing signatures. And then I deposited the check in my carpet-cleaning business account. After a couple of days, the money was available in my account and we split it equally. This was a great thing and we rode it until the wheels fell off.

"I remember that after several weeks, I got a call from a lady at my bank telling me that fraudulent activity had been detected involving my account. The last Marriott check hadn't cleared. She said she wasn't sure of the details, but I was a valued customer and the bank would work with me any way possible to resolve the problem.

"I went to the bank and played the part of the injured party. I said that while the situation was being looked at, I still had my workers to pay. They were counting on their paychecks from me to keep their own bills paid and put food on their tables. What was I supposed to tell them?

"The banker said not to worry about it. She gave me ninety-five hundred in cash to take care of my employees while things were being ironed out. She also told me that I should go to the local police precinct and file a complaint about what had happened to my bank account.

"Taking her advice, I went to the precinct in Bensonhurst to make my report. Most of the guys there knew who I was. It didn't matter, though. I had to do it to cover my tail. They took my complaint, then pretty much laughed me out of the station."

After the scam came to an end, Andrew received regular phone calls from the bank asking him to come in to discuss his account. He never went. One day in late September, he was in a beauty parlor operated by a girl Robert Arena was dating. As he talked with Robert in the rear of the shop, he noticed a familiar figure in one of the chairs getting her hair done. It was none other than the female bank manager who had given him the $9,500 to pay his alleged employees when the Marriott denied payment on the forged check. Their eyes locked. The woman rose from her chair and started toward him. The salon was suddenly a place where Andrew didn't want to be.

"I told Robert that he had to throw a body block on her or do something to stall her until I could make my escape," Andrew laughs as he remembers the meeting. "He intercepted her when she was about halfway to me. He stood in front of her and said how she looked very familiar and wondered where he knew her from. She tried to get around him. But when she stepped to the side, he stepped with her, blocking her path. While they were doing that little dance, I beat it out the back door. I never bumped into her or anyone else from the bank again."

● ● ●

Andrew had made a lot of money from the check scheme and was doing well with his marijuana business. Even though he could have paid Wild Bill Cutolo at least the fifteen thousand dollars back, he refused to give him a dime. To Andrew, it was a matter of principle. He wasn't going to pay money he didn't owe. His relationship with Wild Bill continued to deteriorate. It reached the point that Andrew couldn't attend Billy Cutolo's wedding. That decision opened up yet another issue that Wild Bill would later use against him.

For his problems with the elder Cutolo, Andrew blamed Mike Bolino, who'd defaulted on his loan. And although he liked the guy, he felt he'd been taken advantage of. When the opportunity arose, Andrew decided to repay Bolino in kind.

Mike Bolino approached Robert Arena and Andrew and said he had several hundred pounds of marijuana he wanted to move, and asked if they were interested in helping him unload it. They were. A meeting was set up with one of Mike's partners, who said he'd get the pot to them in a couple of days. A few days later, they met at a diner on 4ᵗʰ Avenue in Bay Ridge, where Andrew gave his car keys to another one of Mike's guys. He drove it away. About twenty minutes later he came back, parked the car in the parking lot, left the keys under the floor mat, and took off.

Andrew and Robert Arena went out to the car. They found two big bales of marijuana in the back seat and the trunk filled with three more, for a total of five hundred pounds. They took off with a friend following in a car behind them. If the cops tried to pull them over, he'd be the crash car, blocking the cops, even if it meant crashing into their vehicle.

"We drove away and within a couple of minutes, two cop cars were running up on us from behind with their sirens blaring. There we were, two organized-crime parolees in possession of a quarter ton of marijuana. That pinch would have been a parole-officer's dream. We didn't know what in the hell to do. Just as the cops got on the bumper of our crash car, they pulled to the right and went on past. I don't know where they were going or who they were after, but it wasn't us. When we came to the next intersection, our buddy pulled side of us. We looked at each other and broke out laughing. The tension was broken and we went on about our business."

Over the next several days, they got rid of all the weed— a hundred pounds here, fifty pounds there. They made about two hundred thousand on the deal.

A few days later, Mike Bolino called asking about payment. That's when Robert and Andrew got back at him for stiffing Andrew on his loan, playing him for a sucker and putting him in a jackpot with Wild Bill. They made up a story that they'd given the stuff to a guy in New Jersey and he'd never gotten back to them. They didn't know what was going on. Basically, they robbed him.

Mike and his guys weren't happy, but they weren't sure where to go with their complaint. It took them a little time to put together a game plan. They went to Nicky Corozzo and Robert's boss, Danny Cutaia. Robert and Andrew both had the green light to rob drug dealers. And they had the approval from their families to work together. They didn't think very much more about it. The money was made and Mike wasn't going to get a penny of it. As far as they were concerned, it was a done deal.

To Andrew and Robert, the bilking of Mike Bolino was a matter of the way business was done on the streets. Bolino had done his friend Andrew wrong and now he'd gotten his payback. That's the way these things worked. However, Andrew and Robert would soon find out that in this particular case, they couldn't have been more wrong.

● ● ●

As Andrew's first full calendar year on parole came to a close, his financial picture was bright. But his organized-crime and personal relationships were another story. Wild Bill Cutolo could be a dangerous enemy and the chasm between him and Nicky Corozzo was widening steadily. He'd also suffered the loss of another one of his crewmates over the summer when Tony "Tough Tony" Placido was gunned down.

On top of those issues, Andrew had begun dating the cousin of his ex-wife Dina. He could almost cut the tension with a knife when he picked up his son for visitation.

But a few weeks into the new year, Andrew would look back at those problems and wish they were all he had to worry about.

16

Beginning of the End

The year 1996 was the most stressful of Andrew DiDonato's life. The pressure cooker he would live in for the next
several months started gaining steam in late January with
the murder of his best friend, Robert Arena. According to
Andrew, the roots of that killing went back to the previous
year's marijuana theft from Mike Bolino and the murder of
Tony Placido.

Tony Placido was part of Nicky's crew. He and Andrew
worked in the horse rooms together and went out looking for
guys once in a while when there was work to do. According to
Andrew, he was a tough kid—real tough. While Andrew was
in Hudson, Tony did time with Robert Arena in Elmira and
they'd become friends. The three of them used to write one
another while we were all locked up. Andrew really liked Tony,
but they weren't as close as he and Robert. And Tony had a
drug problem. When he was high, he had a hair trigger. Sometimes he went out to dinner with friends and by the time the
meal was over, he wanted to kill the people he was with.

That summer, around August, Andrew heard Tony had
been shot dead in the street. Nobody seemed to know who
did it or why. Andrew felt bad and figured that eventually
Nicky would find out what happened. And then if something

needed to be done, it would be done. He didn't give it too much more thought.

But as time went by, more information started coming out. The night Tony was killed, he'd been seen out in Bay Ridge having dinner with Robert Arena. There were a lot of witnesses to that. Then Andrew remembered that he'd gone to Robert's house the morning before Tony's death. He didn't see Robert's car there and asked him about it. He said the car had been stolen sometime overnight. Andrew thought that was strange: Everyone knew who they were and what they did and nobody stole their cars.

"After I left Robert's, I happened to look at a newspaper and read about Tony," Andrew picks up the story. "I didn't connect Robert's car and Tony's murder then. But when it came out that Robert had been the last one seen with Tony, I put two and two together. Robert had killed Tony himself or at least been involved in the murder. He had to ditch his car, which had blood or other evidence in it. As this information came to light, I wasn't the only one to come to that conclusion about Robert. Nicky and the crew did too.

"That could have ended my association with Robert, but it didn't. Our friendship was too strong for that. And I was sure that whatever the reason Tony was killed, it had nothing to do with business. Tony had probably got into the drugs, turned on Robert, and Robert did what he had to do. I wasn't happy about it, but I understood it. I never told Robert what I thought and he never mentioned it either."

Meanwhile, the marijuana deal with Mike Bolino was causing some serious problems as well. The heat on Robert and Andrew from Danny Cutaia and Nicky was intense. Danny had dealers coming to his home, asking for help in getting the marijuana back or getting paid for it. Danny also considered Andrew a threat, perhaps linking his crew to the murder of Tony Placido. Danny wanted Andrew dead and Robert filled him in on the whole plot.

"Although Nicky and me were no longer friends, he was still my boss. I met with him and Mike Yannotti and told them about Danny and what he had planned. It was clear to all of us that unless something changed, it was only a matter of time before our two crews would have an old-fashioned war with guns blazing in the streets. It was at this meeting that Nicky forbid me to do business or hang around with Robert ever again. That was a joke, because Robert was more of a friend to me than my own crew. He could have set me up to be murdered. Instead, he told me what Danny had planned. If that word got back to Danny, Robert would be a dead man himself. He put his life on the line for me."

Several days went by without any excitement. But on a Friday in late January, Andrew got called to Mike Yannotti's house. He'd been summoned by Nicky to commit a murder and Mike needed Andrew. He told Andrew to make himself available for the next twenty-four hours, to respond on a moment's notice. They exchanged beeper and phone numbers and then he left.

Andrew next met up with two other Gambino associates, Tommy Dono and Benny Geritano of the 17th Avenue faction. They planned to intercept a money drop from a local high-end store on 18th Avenue at 86th Street that night.

"The night started off well. Another friend of ours provided us with a minivan he'd stolen from Long Island the night before. The plan called for Tommy and Benny to stay in the van. I was going to be the guy in the street. My job was to wait for the money courier to pass by and push him into the open side door of the van. But as fate would have it, things turned to shit pretty quick.

"Just before we expected the courier to leave the store and walk to the bank in the next block, a cop car pulled a traffic stop on the opposite corner. Then a second car joined him. I was still willing to tackle the courier. But it was a very cold night and when he left the store, he ran to the bank rather than walk. To get him, I'd have had to chase and tackle him in the middle of the street and drag him back to the van. With the cops that close, there was no way. We aborted the robbery. It wasn't that bad, though, because we knew the money run took place every Friday night. So we'd get him the following week or the week after.

"As I look back, it's hard to believe that agreeing to participate in a murder and then attempting a robbery a few hours later were more or less normal for me at that time. Now I realize that kind of thinking and conduct are anything but normal.

"Anyway, after we called off the robbery, we went to get some Japanese food. I called my girlfriend and she met us at this joint on Fourth Avenue. The dinner was great. We had a few drinks and laughs. I checked my beeper every couple of minutes to see if Mike tried to reach me, but there was no word from him. I was ready to head home and as I went out the door, I bumped into Nicky's daughters Bernadette and Donna Marie coming in. I bought them some drinks and made my way out a few minutes later. When I got home, there was still no word from Mike. So I went to sleep with beeper in hand. The next set of events will never leave my memory.

"At approximately five o'clock the next morning, January twenty-seventh, my telephone rang. It wasn't Mike calling me to go to work. It was a childhood friend telling me that Robert Arena and a neighborhood kid named Thomas Maranga had both been shot and killed. They were murdered in Robert's car as he pulled out from a parking space in front of his apartment. The way he described it to me sounded like a massacre. Robert was in the life, but Thomas wasn't. He'd apparently just been in the wrong place at the wrong time.

"I was a tough guy—a gangster. But after I hung up the phone, I cried. I was sad, depressed, and angry all at once. Robert's loss was overwhelming. It left me with a feeling of helplessness. Why did this happen? Why wasn't I there to help my friend like he would have helped me? I asked myself those questions over and over.

"And then it hit me like a bolt of lightning. Mike Yannotti. He and Robert only lived about a block apart. Was Robert the work Mike needed help with? If it was, why hadn't he called me to help like he said? One possibility was that if he included me on the hit, I might have found a way to warn Robert. On the other hand, they could have brought me along and got rid of Robert and me both at the same time. After all, there was no love lost between Nicky and me. He suspected I was holding back money from my scores. To him, I'd become a real pain in the ass.

"At this point, I didn't know who to trust or what to think. I definitely knew that Danny Cutaia wanted me dead. Wild Bill Cutolo was near that point, if he wasn't already there. And maybe Nicky Corozzo had come to the conclusion that his life would be better without me in it. So it was me against the life from that moment on. I'd have to play dumb until I could figure out who was who and what was what.

"I waited an hour, then called Mike Yannotti. I gave him the news about Robert and Thomas as though I didn't connect him to it. I asked him how he thought I should play it. He didn't seem very surprised. I asked if he thought the killings had anything to do with the drug thing Robert and I had been involved in. He wanted to know if Thomas looked like me. I said no. He said he didn't think I had anything to worry about. We arranged a meeting for a few hours later. When I arrived in Brooklyn I called Mike to confirm our meet. He said he couldn't see me then, because the cops were all over the place.

"I drove over anyway to check things out. Sure enough, when I tried to turn the corner to Mike's house, I couldn't. The block was closed off because the cops were still investigating the murders. A radio news report said that Robert was armed at the time, but he didn't fire a shot. The police said

Robert was a known shooter and his failure to use his gun indicated he knew his assailant and was caught by surprise. All things considered, I was becoming convinced that Mike was involved in the killings. He may have acted alone or with help. But there was no doubt in my mind that he was in on it."

Andrew's suspicions about Mike were confirmed the next day when the two men met at Yannotti's apartment. Also present was Nicky Corozzo's son-in-law Vincent Dragonetti and another crew member.

"We talked about the murders and Robert's funeral. Then Mike said to me, 'Listen, Vinny came over to deliver a message from Nicky. We're not goin' to Robert's funeral. He wasn't at Tough Tony's, so we're not goin' to his. But you're gonna go. You and Robert were friends and it would look funny if you didn't show up. So you go and take the temperature. See if anybody asks you anything. And remember, we're denying having anything to do with this to the fullest extent.'

"I said, 'Well, we didn't. Did we?' I knew the only reason we were having this meeting was because we were guilty as hell. I had to keep up my act, though. I didn't expect an answer and I didn't get one.

"After that we talked about how to handle Robert's crew. My relationship had been with Robert; I wasn't that friendly with the rest of them. And of course Danny Cutaia hated me. Mike said that he and I would meet with Nicky in the future to discuss it. For now, Nicky said to sit tight and some plans would be put together in case the situation escalated.

"I walked out of there knowing that my crew had killed Robert. I'd had a hard time controlling my emotions while Mike was feeding me his line of shit. I wanted to shoot him where he stood. But I couldn't. If I tipped my mitt, I was a dead man. So I had to keep myself in check.

"I knew that with nobody else from the crew going to the funeral, word must already be out on the street that we were being blamed for Robert and Thomas.

"They didn't have an actual funeral for Robert. They had a memorial service at Saint Bernard's Church in Bergen Beach. Regina [Dina's cousin], the girl I was dating at the time, had attended school with Robert and they'd been good friends. So the two of us went to the memorial service. We sat down in a pew and I saw the guys from Robert's crew looking at us. We exchanged nods, but their expressions and body language told me what they were thinking. They thought I had a lot of balls showing up at a memorial for a guy that me or my crew had killed.

"After the service, Robert's mother was swarmed by the mourners and I wasn't able to speak with her. I said hello to a couple of the Lucchese guys. They spoke, but barely. Mike had told me to take the temperature. I did and it was ice cold."

● ● ●

Over the next several weeks, more information came to light about Robert's murder. Regina learned from the families of Robert and Thomas that Mike Yannotti's beeper had been found at the scene of the killings. And Andrew learned that Yannotti had been brought in by the police for a voice analysis and to give hair samples for DNA testing. He spoke to Yannotti a couple of times during that period and Yannotti failed to mention that he was a suspect in the case or that his beeper had been recovered at the crime scene.

The more Andrew thought about it, the more he believed Yannotti not calling him to go along on the hit was a clear sign that Nicky Corozzo and Yannotti didn't trust him. But he could only guess at what they were thinking then or now. Then he got more disturbing news.

"The word coming out of the Luccheses and on the street in general was that Mike and I had killed Robert. We were the two shooters. I had an alibi for that night, though. I'd been with Tommy Dono and Benny Geritano on the botched robbery. Then Regina joined us at the Japanese restaurant. After that she went home with me and spent the night. So if I had to, I could have Regina vouch for me that I had nothing to do with Robert's death."

But then things calmed down temporarily when Yannotti left for Florida to let the heat die down.

● ● ●

Andrew returned to his apartment one evening in late February to find a business card under his door. It was from a Secret Service agent. A handwritten note advised Andrew that he was to report to their office at the World Trade Center for a handwriting analysis in the Marriott scam. He wasn't overly concerned about that, because he'd only endorsed the checks, not forged any of the signatures. He contacted Nicky's nephew, attorney Joseph Corozzo Jr., to accompany him.

"The analysis was a piece of cake. Afterward, I took Jo Jo to lunch. I gave him five hundred dollars for his hour of work. He said, 'You can drop the other twenty-five hundred off at my office next week when you get a chance.'

"I almost fell out of my chair. This guy and I had been friends since childhood. And now the bastard wanted to charge me three grand for sitting there while I gave a handwriting sample. I told him, 'Sure. But I might have to be away for a while. If I don't make it into your office before I leave, go see Nicky. Tell him to give you the money for me.'

"I'd told my parole officer about the handwriting thing. He didn't say two words about it at the time. I had to see him again a couple of weeks later. It was on a Wednesday afternoon in the middle of March and everything seemed fine.

"It happened that the same week, I was planning a bank

burglary in Queens with Tommy Dono, Benny Geritano, and some other guys for that Sunday night. We were getting our equipment together and I secured a rental car to use for the job. When I got back to my place Friday afternoon, there was another business card under my door. This one was from my parole officer. He wrote on it that I was to call him as soon as possible. I was surprised, because I'd just seen him two days earlier and everything had been okay. The only thing I could figure was that it had something to do with the Marriott thing.

"I called and he told me that their computer system had crashed and a lot of information was lost. He was updating his files and needed me to come in on Monday. I said sure. But I smelled a rat. I'd been on parole awhile and I'd hung around with parolees all my life. I'd never heard of this happening before. Alarm bells were going off in my head.

"After I hung up, I spent some time trying to figure out what this was all about. The Marriott seemed less likely the more I thought about it. Also, a couple of weeks earlier, I'd been part of a crew that tried to pull a bank burglary in the Bronx. Two of the guys had stolen a piece of heavy equipment to break through the bank's wall. But after we got inside, we weren't able to rip the night-deposit drop out. We had to abort the mission, so it ended up as just some serious vandalism. But I doubted that deal had anything to do with the parole officer wanting to see me. I couldn't think of anything else that would have triggered that phone call. But something wasn't right. I could feel it.

"Under the circumstances, I figured I'd better pass on the Sunday bank job. I got hold of Tommy and Benny. I told 'em I wanted to go on the score, but I didn't want to ruin it if I was hot. The decision was for me to give them the rental car and they'd do the job without me. I'd report to my parole officer on Monday and find out what was up.

"On Monday I went to the parole office. My mother was

now divorced and her boyfriend went with me. We were in the waiting area for about five minutes when my crewmate Mario came in. I told him about having just seen the parole officer the previous Wednesday, but on Friday, he told me I had to come back in.

"Mario said he'd seen some guys that looked like detectives downstairs when he entered the building. They were looking at a file and he thought he heard them mention my name. He said, 'Listen, they can violate us on nothing and hold us on Riker's Island for forty-five days just to bust our balls. If they [the detectives] come up, I think they're gonna violate you. You might wanna get hold of Jo Jo. Have him call in and see what's goin' on.'

"When Mario got called into the office, I told my mother's boyfriend to go out and start the car. He turned white as a sheet, but he went. The door worked by a buzzer, but because he wasn't a parolee, he was able to get right out.

"A few minutes later the two suits came up. They flashed their badges and were buzzed in. As they headed for my parole officer's office, they happened to look over at me. Then they turned and looked at each other like they knew who I was. As they went in the office, the lady at the desk opened the door for another person to come in. Before the door could close, I was gone. I went down the stairs five steps at a time and ran to the car. We drove to my mother's boyfriend's house and I called Jo Jo. I told him what happened and he said to sit tight, he'd get right back to me.

"Jo Jo called back a short time later. He said he'd spoken to the parole officer. He asked him what was going on and said that he wanted to resolve whatever problem there was. The parole officer said he didn't know what Jo Jo was talking about. He'd only say that I was supposed to see him, that I'd been in the office and then ran out. I had until the end of the day to report or I'd be violated. Jo Jo told him that he'd called in good faith to discuss surrender. Since the parole officer was lying to him, there could be no deal. He said they'd have to find me on their own.

"I still didn't know what it was all about. But I sure as hell wasn't going to report in until I did. So from that point, I was officially on the run."

17

Fugitive

So in early 1996, 31-year-old Andrew DiDonato was on the lam, a fugitive from justice for the second time in his life. And the law wasn't all he had to worry about. Factions of the Lucchese and Colombo families wouldn't have been at all unhappy if he were found dead in the trunk of an abandoned car. And some members of his own crew, including the boss, may have felt the same way.

What was it like being pursued by the law and at the same time not knowing if or when one of your own might put a couple in your head? "Take your most stressful day and multiply it by ten thousand. And then by ten thousand more. That's what it's like being hunted and not knowing who you can trust—and that your first misstep will probably be your last."

Staying free and keeping alive cost money, lots of it. Andrew began preparing for living as a fugitive as soon as he received the bad news from his lawyer, Jo Jo Corozzo.

"When I hung up the phone from Jo Jo, I reached out to Tommy Dono and Benny Geritano and set up a meet. When we got together, they said the bank job had been successful. They gave me my end of the score and the rental car, so I could return it. I told them about the parole deal and that I didn't know what the hell was goin' on. They told me to lie low until I could find out what kind of trouble I was in. Benny said I'd be able to contact him through his grandmother.

"Next I stopped at Fat Sal's [Salvatore "Fat Sal" Mangiavillano] pizza joint near Riker's Island. Fat Sal was a part of our bank crew that later became known as the 'Night Drop Crew.' He was an electronics guy and a wizard at disabling alarms. He and I both received full ends of the bank score even though neither of us were physically there. I told him about my problem and that I'd need to make some good scores in order to survive. He said not to worry about it, that we'd keep busy."

Andrew initially believed he'd be able to generate enough money to cover the additional expenses he'd incur while being on the run. These included hotel and apartment rents, eating most meals out, and compensating people who helped him with temporary lodging or in other ways. But about two weeks later, an incident took place that struck very close to home and caused him to take a second look at the effect living the life was having on the person who loved him the most.

"My girlfriend Regina's father was with the Genovese family and was incarcerated in a medium-security federal prison at the time. He knew that I was dating his daughter and I'd previously gotten his approval to marry her. One day in early April, I was visiting one of my sisters when Regina called. She said that one of her father's friends, a guy named Charlie, had contacted her. He told her he needed to meet with me to deliver a message from her dad. Even though I was trying to avoid exposing myself to danger unnecessarily, out of respect for her father I said okay. But in my world, a person's life was often taken by someone he trusted, someone he thought was his friend. With that in mind, I said the get-together would have to be on my terms. I wouldn't call Charlie with the time and location of the meeting until the last possible minute. If he had bad intentions, I wasn't going to give him enough advance notice to put together a plan.

"A few days later I was again at my sister's place and my mother was with me. I called Charlie and told him to meet me right away on Ocean Parkway in Brooklyn. This is a busy six-lane street with lots of vehicle and pedestrian traffic. There were benches on either side of the road where people could sit, relax, and make small talk. I hung up the phone and was on my way.

"Charlie showed up alone and we sat on one of the benches and talked. He told me that word had reached Regina's father in prison that I was in trouble with factions of the Colombo and Lucchese families. No one knew how far things might escalate. There was a possibility that I would be assassinated or a war could break out between them and my own crew. On top of that, the law was after me. And with my reputation for violence, they might shoot first and ask questions later. Like any caring father, he didn't want his daughter to be in harm's way. For that reason, he wanted me to stop dating her.

"I listened to Charlie closely and completely understood where Regina's father was coming from. And then out of the corner of my eye I saw a woman sitting on the bench twenty feet away holding a handgun in her lap. It was my mother. If I could see the gun, so would Charlie if he looked in that direction. And if Charlie made any moves my mother thought posed a danger to me, she might come after him. If that happened, he'd probably try to defend himself and I'd have had no choice but to kill him. I quickly assured Charlie he could tell Regina's father I wouldn't see her again. I kept talking so his eyes stayed focused on me as I walked him to his car.

"When he was gone, I returned to the bench where my mother was sitting. I was angry. What the fuck did she think she was doing? But as I got closer, the anger turned to sadness as I saw her trembling and crying. We hugged and she literally collapsed in my arms.

"When she was able to talk, she admitted that she'd eavesdropped on my phone conversation with Charlie. She was afraid that I was being set up. She knew that I kept guns stashed around the various places I frequented. So as soon as I left my sister's, she took one of the guns and followed me to the meet.

"My life had just reached an all-time low. It really hit home that the way I'd been living all these years was devastating my family. Here was my mother out on the street carrying a gun—ready to do murder to protect me. I think it was that moment that ultimately opened my eyes that being a part of this cancer called the Gambino crime family could never have a happy ending for anybody."

● ● ●

While Andrew realized his chosen lifestyle was having a devastating effect on his mother, there didn't seem to be a great deal he could do about it. He couldn't simply throw away his guns and become a legitimate working man. He was facing as-yet unknown legal issues and his criminal colleagues weren't exactly the let-bygones-be-bygones types. If he wanted to stay free and alive, it required a good and steady income. And in Andrew's shoes, that meant he had to continue his criminal activities. It didn't take him long to figure out a new angle that would greatly improve his financial position.

"A couple weeks after the incident with my mother on Ocean Parkway, I met up with an old friend I hadn't seen in a while. He said he knew a guy who had a solid connection with a marijuana supplier from California. This guy could get five or ten pounds of marijuana shipped in at a time and it would provide a steady income. He gave me the guy's phone number. I made contact with him and we opened up a business.

"Here's how we set it up. The weed was mailed from California to New York. We got the tracking number of the package and gave it to an accomplice working in a management position at the post office. He intercepted it and turned it over to us. We did a trial run with five pounds of marijuana. It worked perfectly and we started receiving regular shipments.

"With a steady income, I didn't have to rely on my friends as much. I used some of the money to rent an apartment in Manhattan Beach in Brooklyn. Although Regina and me had stopped seeing each other, she put the apartment in her name. Nobody else knew I was living there and I never invited anybody over. It was my safe house.

"I continued to get word that Wild Bill Cutolo wasn't happy with me. And Danny Cutaia and his crew were still pointing fingers at Mike Yannotti and me for Robert Arena's murder. This stuff was causing a lot of stress, so I reached out to Nicky Corozzo. I asked him what I should do if I ran into one of those guys. First, he said no decision had been made about how to handle the Cutaia faction—whether to eliminate the whole crew, take them out one at a time, or what. There was nothing firm, but murder was in the air.

"He then explained the rules that were in effect until then. If I met them in a neutral area, I could only react to defend myself. If I saw them in a danger zone, I could shoot to kill without waiting for them to make the first move. A danger zone was around my mother's or my sisters' homes, where my son was living, or anywhere I was laying my head at night. If anybody came around those locations, they undoubtedly had bad intentions.

"I had a meet with Mike to discuss the whole situation. I told him it was nearing critical mass. I'll never forget what he said to me. He said that if they came for me, it was only because they were going to clean house. He said he was the one who had to worry. And then he openly admitted that he had killed Robert. Even though I'd figured he was involved, hearing it from his own mouth was a blow to me. I was so angry I wanted to shoot him right there and then. But I had to bite my tongue and act like it didn't bother me. If he saw my emotions, he'd have felt justified in killing me. And this wasn't the time for a shootout. I figured there'd be another time down the line."

• • •

Andrew now had two issues of revenge on the back burner: Sammy Karkis and Mike Yannotti. The timing wasn't right to take action in either case. But a third man seemed intent on forcing the fugitive gangster's hand.

"My sister was in a bad way. She wasn't the woman that I remembered from before I went to prison. My brother-in-law had done a number on her physically and emotionally. Her kids had seen some bad things go down in the house. When I warned him to clean up his act or get out of her life, I thought he got the message. He didn't. The abuse continued. I thought it was time for him to go.

"Following protocol, I contacted Mike Yannotti, went to his house, and told him what I wanted to do. He said he'd run it past Nicky and see if he'd give his approval for the hit. Mike was already personally on board with the idea. We talked some more and developed a plan for the killing.

"My brother-in-law was an electrician. He respected and feared Mike. I knew that if Mike called him and said he needed some electrical work done at his house, he'd show up fast. He wouldn't dare not to. When he arrived, Mike would have him pull his truck into the garage that was under the house and kill him there. We'd then get rid of his body and the truck. He'd just disappear and no one would ever know if he was dead or alive. We decided to do a dry run. I followed Mike down the stairs that led to the garage. It was pitch black—a perfect place for a killing.

"In a day or two, Mike got back to me and said Nicky had given me the green light to do the killing as long as it didn't come back on the crew. For the first time in my life, I knew what it was like to hold that ultimate power. This wasn't something I was ordered to do by someone else. It was my decision, and my decision alone, whether my brother-in-law lived or died.

"Mike told me that it was all up to me. If I wanted to go forward with the plan, he'd make the call to my brother-in-law right away, get him over there, and be done with it. But he suggested I think it over some more before I made up my mind. He pointed out that it wasn't just my sister involved. She'd lose a husband, but the kids would also lose their father. If the truth ever became known or suspected by my family, the kids could end up hating me.

"Those were good points and I agreed to think about it. It was a very hard decision for me to make, because I couldn't stand the thought of my sister being in pain and I knew he'd inflicted a lot of it on her. But in the end, I spared his life. I had the power of life and death in my hands and I chose to let him live. I gave him his walking papers and let it go.

"Looking back at it today, do I think it was the right decision? My sister still has emotional scars from what he put her through and it hurts me to see that. But their daughter was married recently and he was invited to the wedding. That makes me feel confident that I did the right thing.

"That experience gave me an insight into what it's like to be an organized-crime boss—to have that kind of power over other people's very lives. Just imagine having the ability to determine who lives and who dies. When those guys become bloodthirsty because their egos get the best of them, or maybe they're mentally unbalanced, look at the destruction they can cause. It's kind of a scary thought, isn't it?"

● ● ●

As the summer of 1996 approached, Andrew found himself in dire financial trouble. His California marijuana connection proved to be less reliable than it first appeared and that income was inconsistent. Unable to commit street crimes as he had in the past, he was bringing in only enough money to pay his basic expenses and pick up a cheap car to get him from place to place. His already-grim situation was growing steadily grimmer.

"My ex-wife was always looking for more money for our son's support. Wild Bill Cutolo was still insisting that I pay back a bogus loan. And Danny Cutaia was beating the war drums, saying that I'd been involved in Robert Arena's murder. That scenario was the most hurtful because I would have done anything in my power to save Robert, even if it had meant dying with him and going out in a blaze of glory. So being accused of killing him was a hard pill to swallow.

"Around that time, I started seeing a girl named Charlotte. She was the niece of Greg "The Grim Reaper" Scarpa. He was a capo in the Colombo family and ran one of the most notorious crews in organized-crime circles. Greg had died a couple of years earlier and Charlotte and her aunt used to tell me a lot of stories about him. She was smart and knew how to keep a secret. We hit it off really well and before long she became my close friend as well as a love interest. We were almost inseparable.

"One day I got a beeper message from a Genovese bank-robbery crew I knew. There was a potential score coming up and they wanted me to take a look at it. It involved robbing a specific Brinks armored truck that operated out of the yard in downtown Brooklyn. The information was that if we robbed the truck around Christmas time, it would be carrying around three million dollars. I met up with [notorious bank robber associated with the Bonano family] Paul Mazzarese. Paul was older and grandfatherly looking, but he knew his stuff when it came to banks. Paul and me picked up that truck when it left the yard and followed it all day. Afterward, we talked about it. Paul said that he had an idea for something we could do a lot sooner than Christmas. That interested me, because in my financial situation, I didn't think I could last that long.

"Paul lived in New Jersey. He cashed his checks at a Sovereign Bank branch. He noticed that the Brinks money truck came every Thursday and dropped off bags of money. But the procedure was lax: The bags were left on the floor next to the vault until an employee got around to putting them inside. And there was no partition in that facility between the customers and tellers. You could get to the money bags by simply jumping over the counter.

"So we switched our focus from robbing the armored truck in Brooklyn to taking down the bank in New Jersey. Our plan was for four of us—Paul, Tommy Scuderi, Joe Miraglia, and me—to do the robbery on the Thursday before a holiday weekend. I knew from doing bank burglaries that they usually brought in a hundred and fifty thousand or so more than usual then to fill the ATM machines for the long weekend. The next upcoming holiday with a three-day weekend was Labor Day."

The week before Labor Day, the four of them waited at a diner along the highway for the truck to pass and followed it to the bank to get the timing down. They then bought some tape the same color as the letters and numbers on their license plates so they could cover the real letters and numbers with fakes.

The Wednesday before the robbery, they went to the bank for a final look. Paul explained everyone's job one last time. He lived in a senior-citizen complex exactly 60 seconds from the bank. He'd drive Tommy and Andrew to the bank and park in the lot where they could keep an eye out for the Brinks truck. After it arrived, Tommy and Andrew would get out of Paul's car and go inside to do the robbery.

Paul would then drive around behind the bank and wait for them. Joe would be in a car across the street monitoring a police scanner. As the up-front man, Andrew would walk in first, followed by Tommy a few seconds later. Andrew would go straight to the counter, jump over, and grab the money bags on the floor next to the vault. Tommy would wait at the counter and help him carry the bags out and handle any uncooperative employees or customers. After they got the money, they'd hop in Paul's car and drive to his place. Joe would follow close behind. Then they'd all wait there until the heat died down.

"That night I sat in my apartment in Manhattan Beach and said a little prayer before I went to bed. A bank robber's prayer. I said, 'Lord, things haven't been too good lately. And I would never pray for you to help me steal. But I'm going to do what I'm going to do tomorrow and I'm asking you to watch over me.'"

The next morning, Andrew got up early, was picked up by Tommy and Joe, and drove to Paul's. After doctoring the license plates, they left for the bank. They'd done a dry run of the escape route the night before and were ready to do the job. Like clockwork, the Brinks truck pulled in within an hour after the bank opened. And just like they figured, there were two extra bags of money for the holiday. The guard loaded the bags on a hand cart and wheeled them into the bank. Back outside in a couple of minutes, he got into the truck and drove away.

"I exited Paul's car followed by Tommy and we headed for the bank. I had on doctor's-exam gloves and a sweatshirt that covered a bulletproof vest, sunglasses, and a New York Yankees ball cap. The bank had four or five customers at the time. I kept my head straight, went directly to the counter, and jumped over it. I heard a couple of screams, but kept my focus on the money bags. I grabbed the first two and threw them over the counter to Tommy. Then I took the other two bags and jumped back over the counter. Some guy decided to be a hero and made a move at me. Tommy pulled his handgun, grabbed the guy, and threw him on the floor. There must have been a lot of wax on the floor, because the guy slid quite a distance.

"At that time, a female customer came in and saw what was happening. She started screaming and ran outside. Tommy and I followed her out and went behind the bank. We threw the bags into Paul's car, got in, and laid down on the back seat. As Paul pulled away, he'd have looked to any passersby like a grandfather out driving around all alone. We were safely inside Paul's house in just about a minute after the robbery and Joe was right behind us.

"The traffic on the police scanner was that they were responding to a bank robbery and that roadblocks were being set up. They were also reporting that the robbers were a male and female team, because witnesses had seen me follow the screaming female customer outside. The cops pulled her over a block away and took her in for questioning. After a while, they figured out she wasn't involved.

"I'd worked out an arrangement with Charlotte for me to contact her by beeper to let her know how the score went. If it was successful, I was to beep her one-four-three. In beeper lingo, that meant 'I love you.' I sent her the message, then shaved and took a shower, and everybody changed clothes. We bagged up our robbery clothes and gear and Paul's wife disposed of everything. After that we counted the loot. The take was just under a half-million dollars. We split it four ways. Tommy and Joe had to take care of Sal DeMeo [their crew boss] from their end. According to protocol, I was supposed to kick some of my share up to Nicky. I didn't, though. At least not right away.

"We stayed at Paul's for several hours, eating, listening to the scanner, and watching the news. When we felt it was safe, Paul's wife drove me back to Staten Island. Tommy and

Joe followed in Joe's car with our money in the trunk. In Staten Island, I got in with Joe and Tommy and they drove me to my apartment in Manhattan Beach. I took my end of the score and we agreed to meet later that night and take Sal DeMeo out to dinner.

"After they left, I went to a pay phone around the corner from my place and called my mother. I told her to take a cab straight from work and meet me. When she got there, we grabbed another cab to her house. I put almost all of my money—a hundred thousand dollars—into her clothes hamper. I only kept a few dollars for myself.

"When the robbery crew met up later, we took Sal to a restaurant in Bay Ridge. Sal was a great guy and his guys really liked him. They chipped in five thousand apiece to him. We had a nice dinner and did some talking. Sal said he had a friend who owned his own armored-car service. He'd bid on a job and promised that if he got the bid, he'd provide us with the key to the vault and we could empty it out. We had our fingers crossed for the next two weeks that this guy would get the bid. But he didn't, so we had to look elsewhere."

● ● ●

In late September, Andrew received a phone call from Mike Yannotti. He said they needed to meet, so he could relay some messages from Nicky Corozzo. When the two men got together, Andrew found that Yannotti seemed to have developed a slightly different attitude toward him and his situation.

The first thing Mike told him was that the problem with Wild Bill Cutolo needed to be resolved. Mike and Nicky had heard about the New Jersey bank robbery and that Andrew had some cash. According to their thinking, it was time for him to settle the account with Wild Bill.

Andrew told Mike that he didn't owe Wild Bill all the

money he claimed was owed. He refused to admit that his son had blown some of the stash he'd left and he was trying to get it back out of Billy's friends. He wasn't going to let Wild Bill shake him down and he didn't care how pissed off he got.

"The next day Mike called me again and said he needed to see me right away. I went to his house and he said that he thought it was better if we talked outside. We'd go out through the garage in case anyone was watching the house. As I followed him down the steps, I remembered our dry run when we were planning to kill my brother-in-law. My heart started to race. I pulled the gun from my waistband and held it inches from the back of Mike's head. If I was about to meet the same fate as Robert Arena, Mike wouldn't be around to brag about it. At the first sign of a trap, he was a dead man. But as we entered the garage, enough light came in from around the overhead door that I could see we were alone. I put my gun away. When Mike reads this book—and I know he will—it will be the first time he'll know what could have happened that day.

"After we got out to the back yard, Mike said that he and Nicky were considering killing Danny Cutaia. If they decided to do it, they'd want me to be a part of it. Then he went back to the Wild Bill situation and that it had to be taken care of.

"And then he said something that confirmed what I already thought. My problems with the parole people were related to Robert Arena's murder. Regina had been telling me things she heard from Robert's family. The cops thought I was involved and it was said the two detectives that came to the parole office that day were from Homicide. Like it or not, I was a suspect. Mike suggested that I turn myself in. He figured when they questioned me, they'd tip their hand as to how strong their evidence was and what kind of case they were building against him.

"I told him that I was doing better than I had in a long time. And I was. I had the cash from the bank score, was driving a brand new Mercedes, and I'd resurrected my deal with the marijuana dealer in California. Money was starting to come in on a regular basis. And because I was on the run, it gave me an excuse not to have to see Nicky as much. I said that law enforcement was going to have to earn their money and catch me.

"When I left Mike's, I figured he wasn't very happy with what I'd told him. And I was pretty sure that trip down through the cellar was part of a setup. The next time, we wouldn't be alone. I knew I had to take stock of what the future held and how much time I had before Wild Bill, Danny Cutaia, or Nicky made their move. Even that line about killing Danny could have been bullshit to keep me on the reservation. For all I knew, the three of them might be plotting together to get rid of me."

● ● ●

Shortly after his meeting with Mike Yannotti, Andrew decided to seek some stress relief by taking Charlotte and her daughter to Florida to visit Disney World. He figured a few days there would allow him to get his thoughts together and plan for the future. As he was preparing for the trip, he contacted his local marijuana connection to tell him he'd be out of town.

The connection told him he had a buddy who might be able to help him out with false identification. When they got together, the friend told Andrew he had blank California birth certificates, blank Social Security cards, and a UPS photo identification card that could show Andrew was an employee.

They filled out all the necessary information, then drove out to a Department of Motor Vehicles office on Long Island. Andrew applied for a driver's license under the name of Joseph Conti, the name of his mother's boyfriend. He took the written test and made an appointment for a road test. Before he left, they issued him a non-driver identification card.

"My Mercedes was registered and insured in Joseph Conti's name. To get by until my road test, I had Conti tell DMV he lost his license and needed a replacement. At that time they sent a non-photo license right away, followed a few days later by the real license. I took the non-photo license. It happened that I got stopped at a drunk-driving checkpoint. I showed my paperwork and got waved on with no questions asked.

"Within a month, I had a brand new driver's license as Joseph Conti. A lot of guys in the life who are on the run get caught for stupid things, like driving without a license or not having proper identification. That was one less worry for me. I gave my guy a couple hundred for the fake identification and put him to work in my marijuana business."

● ● ●

After the trip to Disney World, Andrew took another getaway jaunt to San Diego. While he was there, he just rested and didn't conduct any business. However, back in New York, his marijuana partner came up with another way to enhance their operation and profits.

Andrew's associate had a friend who drove a tractor-trailer to California every 10 days. Their San Diego connection could load the truck and start sending product back that way. It sounded like a good deal and they entered into negotiations to set it up.

While he was waiting to put the new delivery system into effect, Andrew snuck a visit to one of his sisters. He parked about a block and a half away and started walking toward her place. When he rounded the corner of 58th Street and Avenue N, he saw two guys standing on the street talking: Wild Bill Cutolo and Danny Cutaia.

"Here I was on the run from the law and I bumped into my two biggest organized-crime enemies. What were the odds of bosses from two different families having a conversation on a street corner at the very same time a guy they hated walked by? Wild Bill saw me and said, 'Well, look who just walked into the lion's mouth.' I answered that it would mean somethin' if the fuckin lion had any teeth. An argument ensued.

"Wild Bill said, 'Listen, you motherfucker. You owe me money and I want it. I'm gonna go to Nicky and Lenny. If they don't go to bat for you, you're gonna have a big fuckin' problem. Do you understand that?'

"If I hadn't been so stressed, I might have handled the situation differently. I had a lot of respect for Wild Bill and I loved Billy. Only a year or so earlier, I wanted to transfer to his crew. But on that day I said to him, 'You listen to me and you listen good. I've got the FBI, the cops, and the parole people looking for me. And I've got this cocksucker's [Danny Cutaia] family looking for me. You're the last person I'm worried about.'

"He said, 'You'd better listen to what I'm sayin' or I'll put you in the fuckin' ground.'

"I told him, 'I heard ya. You go to Nicky and Lenny. And if they don't go to bat for me, do you think that makes me more dangerous to you or less dangerous? As far as puttin' me in the fuckin' ground, why don't you try it right here and right now?'

"At that point Danny Cutaia cut in. He warned me that I was out of line. He said, 'You're on thin ground here.'

"I said, 'Mind your own business, you motherfucker. You think I don't know what your plan is? You couldn't kill me on your best day, you bastard.'

"As I walked away, Wild Bill was still hollering threats. I started laughing and kept on going. It wasn't funny, though. I'd challenged bosses from two other families. And that wasn't allowed. If I'd put my hands on either of them, Nicky and Lenny would have had to go along with my murder. That was the resolution required under Mob protocol. But a verbal confrontation didn't mean an automatic death sentence.

"Wild Bill didn't waste much time makin' his beef. Within five days, I got word that Mike Yannotti was looking for me to tell me I had to come in for a meet with Nicky. I called Mike and told him I was out of town and would be away for a couple of weeks.

"In early December, I arranged to meet with Nicky, Lenny, and some of the crew at a diner on Flatbush Avenue. When I got there, I bullshitted with the guys. They seemed glad to see me and said they couldn't believe how long I'd been able to stay on the run. I made a joke of it. I said that if I'd known life on the run was going to be so good, I'd have done it years earlier.

"After about five minutes of that, Nicky got down to business. He said he called the meeting because there were a lot of things to discuss. The first thing was the Wild Bill situation. He told me to explain to Lenny what was going on. I went through the whole deal, right up to the thing on the street corner.

"When I finished, Lenny reminded me that if I ever touched Wild Bill or Danny, there was nothin' he or Nicky could do for me. They'd have to give me up—I'd have to die.

"I said Wild Bill treated me like a fuckin' mutt. If he was doin' that to me, what was he sayin' about them?

"Lenny thought it over a few seconds. Then he said he liked my story better than Wild Bill's. He wanted me to pick him up later that afternoon and we'd go to Wild Bill's social club and resolve the matter once and for all. I said okay.

"After that, Nicky asked me about the bank robberies. I said I didn't know what he was talkin' about. He said he knew about the New Jersey job and wanted to know where his money was. I told him I was on the run and needed every dime I could get my hands on. But I promised to send some money to him the next week. That seemed to satisfy him.

"Next he said he was gonna make some changes. He wasn't sure what to do with me. He was thinking about having me work directly with Mike Yannotti or Lenny. He said he was leaning toward Lenny. I remember thinking how great it would be if I went with Lenny. You could talk to him like a friend. With Nicky, it was all Mob all the time. He was like a machine. Getting away from him would be the best thing that could happen for me.

"I asked him why he was making these changes. He said he was stepping up. That meant he was taking over as boss of the Gambino family. And in the life, the boss can't have his own crew, because it would show favoritism. So he said he was putting me with Lenny and Mike would be my go-between.

"With that out of the way, Nicky said he had some serious law-enforcement problems. The feds were after him and his taking over the family would double the speed of their investigation. He expected to be arrested at any time. But even with that hanging over his head, the door was open for him and he had to grab the opportunity. After all, that was what every gangster who came up from the streets dreamed of being some day: the boss of the family.

"Nicky turned to me and made the sign of a gun with his thumb and finger. He said if he did get arrested, there'd be a lot of work [killing] to do. Then he looked around at everybody and he said, 'Do you hear me? I said if I get arrested, there's gonna be a lot of fuckin' work to do.'

"Nicky grabbed my hand and said, 'And we're gonna start with that fuckin' Baby Huey in Queens.' Baby Huey was what we called Junior Gotti. Nicky looked at me and Mike Yannotti. He said, 'Okay. Start gettin' familiar with this guy.' Mike nodded. I said sure, whatever had to be done would be done. Nicky said he'd contact me later by beeper and we'd get together. Then the meeting ended.

"Two hours later, Lenny and me drove to the sit-down at Wild Bill's social club. Lenny told me to wait outside while he went in and talked with Wild Bill. He said he was going to settle the problem, but not use his new position in the Gambino family to abuse him. That meant to me that with Nicky's rise to boss, Lenny was probably going to be the underboss.

"Lenny was gone for about an hour. When he came back he said, 'You know, this guy hates your fuckin' guts. But he agreed to settle your debt for seven thousand. Get it to him as soon as you can. So as of now, this thing is squashed. You watch out for yourself anyway, though.'

"I asked him if this was squashed, why I had to still be careful. I mean, for the time being Nicky and Lenny were two of the most powerful gangsters in New York. Wild Bill was just a crew boss. If they said the beef was squashed, it should have been squashed.

"Lenny said he wasn't talking about Wild Bill. He wouldn't elaborate, but he gave me a warning. 'I don't want ya' to get caught with your dick in your hand. Don't trust nobody. Not even in your own backyard, kid.'

"Was Lenny telling me that Nicky was getting ready to give the order to have me whacked? Would Mike Yannotti be the assassin? I didn't know and he didn't say. But that statement put me on a serious red alert. When I dropped Lenny off, he gave me one more piece of advice. 'If they start calling you in [for meetings] too many times, do yourself a favor and don't go after a while.'

"By the end of that day, I felt I had no choice but to continue to keep an eye on Wild Bill, who was still upset with me over the money deal. I knew how Danny Cutaia felt about me. And from what Lenny had told me, I wasn't in very good shape with Nicky either. I was already being very careful. How much more cautious could I be?

"Nicky wanted to meet with me again about a week later. But before that took place, he was arrested on federal racketeering charges in Key Biscayne, Florida."

● ● ●

On December 18, 1996, Nicky Corozzo was arrested on charges of attempted murder, loansharking, and racketeering. A newspaper report of the arrest said Corozzo was nabbed by federal agents as he emerged from a swim in the Atlantic Ocean at the Sonesta Beach Hotel in Key Biscayne, shortly before he was to depart for New York City. Officials said the arrest was certain to create even more disarray in the Gambino crime family.

The arrest coincided with the unsealing of a 20-count indictment that accused Corozzo of an array of charges, including running the Gambino gang's crime activities in South Florida for at least four years, operating a vast loansharking ring that charged extortionate interest rates up to 260% a year, and arson.

Investigators said that Corozzo was believed to have succeeded John Gotti as the godfather of the Gambino family after leaders in the city's four other Mafia factions—the Genovese, Lucchese, Colombo, and Bonanno families—demanded that Gotti step down. They'd complained that Gotti, serving a life sentence for murder and racketeering, could no longer effectively run the Gambino group from a cell in the federal penitentiary in Marion, Illinois.

Also indicted on racketeering charges with Corozzo was Leonard DiMaria, who officials said was Corozzo's right-hand man and had recently taken command of Corozzo's old Brooklyn crew. DiMaria was arrested by the FBI at his home in Flatlands, Brooklyn.

The indictment by a federal grand jury in Fort Lauderdale asserted that Corozzo had ordered the abduction and murder of an associate in the family, Louis Maione, suspected of stealing $20,000 from the loansharking operation. Investigators said the FBI had been investigating the Florida crew for two years and that its loansharking activities were conducted through a front, the E-Z Check Cashing Company in Deerfield Beach, a town near Fort Lauderdale.

From wiretaps, the FBI learned about the alleged conspiracy to murder Maione, who cooperated with the inquiry after agents warned him that his life was in danger.

Although Nicky had predicted his arrest days earlier, it still sent shockwaves through the crew.

"We couldn't believe it happened so quick," Andrew recalls. "I started to wonder that if they were that close to Nicky, were there agents in the diner when we had our meeting? Did they know about me? How safe was my safe house? I wasn't sure what to do. I didn't want to give up my apartment and go back to living like a gypsy.

"A few days later, I got a call from Lenny. He'd been pinched with Nicky, but had been able to arrange bail. Nicky hadn't. Lenny wanted to know how long before I was going to get Wild Bill his seven thousand. I had the money, but I asked him to give me a few days. Then he told me that Nicky expected me to help him with his lawyer fees. I told him I'd help him if he needed it. But Nicky had millions. Why in the fuck should I help him?

"Lenny said that with all the law-enforcement pressure, nobody could earn like before. Everybody had to tighten their belt. He even told me I had the green light to bring my associates in the drug business forward and put them on record [introduce them to the crew boss].

"Selling drugs was supposedly taboo in organized crime. All the families made money from drugs, but they claimed they earned from shaking down the dealers, not from dealing themselves. I'd been around the Gambino family all my adult life and I'd never been given a green light to bring drug dealers forward. Something wasn't right. If they wanted to know who my dealers were, it was because they were going to pass them on to somebody else. Which meant I probably wasn't going to be around.

"Nicky wanted me to set up a hit on Junior Gotti, bring my drug connections forward, and pay his legal fees. It didn't take a rocket scientist to figure out they were measuring me up for a casket myself. All the signs were there. The dry run at Mike Yannotti's house. Lenny's warning about being careful in my backyard. The notice that a lot of work would be done after Nicky went to jail.

"I'd also found out from my Genovese bank-robbery crew that after my last meeting with Nicky, he'd sent Vinny Dragonetti around to find out how much we'd made on the New Jersey score. They stonewalled him and said they didn't know what he was talkin' about. I could only imagine how much that must have pissed him off.

"And in the Junior Gotti thing, it wasn't uncommon in a high-profile hit to get rid of the shooter afterward. Lenny got arrested on additional charges right after that and his bail was revoked. I wasn't able to see or talk with him again.

"About a week later, I ran into a guy with a street name of Black Dom from Wild Bill's crew. I knew him and liked him. He said he had a message for me from Wild Bill: Nobody had come forward with the seven thousand yet. I told him to tell his boss that gettin' him or anybody else killed trying to collect seven grand wasn't very smart. Dom knew that even though I liked him, I'd shoot him right there if he tried anything. He said, 'Andrew, I've got no problem with you. I'm not even gonna tell Wild Bill I saw you.'

"I felt like I was on life support—in a kill-or-be-killed situation. I wore a bulletproof vest whenever I was out on the street and was armed to the teeth. My friends thought I had dementia, because I was no longer on time for appointments. If a meeting was scheduled for six, I showed up at seven. If I was supposed to call somebody on Monday, they heard from me on Wednesday. I did everything with the intent of not letting anybody pin down my movements. If I established any patterns, it would probably cost me my life. Each and every day I waited for the shoe to drop."

● ● ●

As 1997 began, the pressure on Andrew increased regarding his personal safety. But his financial situation improved as he finalized the marijuana operation with his San Diego connection. He and his partner put in $100,000 to cover setup expenses. His partner and their new associate, the guy who had prepared his fake identification, traveled to Las Vegas to get things moving. Andrew stayed in New York to receive the shipments.

Marijuana came in from Mexico to San Diego. It went from there to Las Vegas on the friend's tractor-trailer. In Vegas the load was broken down and shipped to Brooklyn by UPS and a private trucking company. On the first run, they got about five hundred pounds. The second time yielded about three hundred. But on the third or fourth trip, the fake-document guy got pinched in Vegas with about 150 pounds of marijuana and around $65,000 in cash. And that was the end of the marijuana business.

"My partner told me that we needed to bail the guy out right away; otherwise he might start cooperating with the law. We got him out a few days later. A short time afterward, my partner was implicated in that same drug deal and was arrested in Vegas as well. When he got out on bail, they both returned to New York. I met them at my partner's house to discuss the case against them and what we could do to help with their legal fees.

"I had suspicions from the start about the way this thing had come down. I couldn't put my finger on it, but alarm bells were going off in my head big time about these two guys. When I went to the meeting, I even considered killing them both right there. But that was a spur-of-the-moment thought. I had no plan in place. My car was parked on the street and I didn't know if they'd told anybody else about the meeting.

"The decision not to kill them turned out to be a wise one, as I found out later on. And that was the last meeting I had with them."

● ● ●

As winter turned to spring, Andrew was living in a shell and maintained regular contact only with Charlotte and the members of the bank-robbery crew, as they were planning another score. He lived a day at a time and made no long-range plans. As each day dawned, he didn't know if he'd have to take someone's life or if someone would try to take his. And, of course, the law was still anxious to catch up with him.

"They were stressful, stressful times," Andrew recalls. "Around April Mike Yannotti reached out to me and wanted to meet. We talked about Junior Gotti. We'd never received the order from Nicky to carry out the hit. Junior had been arrested in February and was still behind bars. It didn't look like he stood much chance of getting bail, so there didn't seem to be a great deal we could do about him for the moment. Mike tried to get me to another meeting later on, but I didn't show.

"On the morning of May seventh, me and the Genovese guys had plans to rob the same bank in New Jersey. They hadn't changed their procedures after the first robbery and we figured they'd never expect us to come back. But we had to postpone the job until I came up with the stolen license plates we needed to put on our cars. I planned to do a dry run that morning, though, just to make sure there hadn't been any last-minute changes at the bank or on the escape route, like road construction.

"Charlotte picked me up at my apartment at ten o'clock, driving my Mercedes. She came into the basement apartment and I remember asking her about the weather. She said it was nice, so I put on a light jacket. I locked my door and we took two steps up to the street level. And then all I could hear was racing car engines and squealing tires. I looked to my left and saw a minivan approaching with the side door already sliding open. I shoved Charlotte into the bushes next to us and started to run down the driveway. I saw two men running toward me from my back yard. I ran up on the stoop, thinking I could jump over the fence. Then one of the men coming at me from the back yard pulled a chain up from around his neck with a badge on it. When I saw the badge, I stopped dead in my tracks. I thought, it's the law; I can handle this. I breathed a little sigh of relief and surrendered.

"The arresting officers were part of a joint task force made up of FBI agents, New York State Police, NYPD, and state parole. They took me back in my apartment, put me up against the wall, and searched me and my apartment. They found all kinds of guns. There was a Mossberg pump riot shotgun, a Baretta nine millimeter, a thirty-eight-caliber revolver, a machine gun, and three hundred rounds of ammunition.

"During the search I overheard two of the parole guys talking. One of them told the other that when I surrendered on the stoop, I pulled my jacket back. He thought I was going for a gun and came very close to shooting me. I had pulled my jacket back, but only to show I wasn't armed. He was pretty nerved up over what had almost happened. I remember his hand was still shaking when they transported me to the precinct.

"An investigator named Tom Scanlon searched my wallet and pulled my Joseph Conti driver's license out of it. There was no doubt he already knew it was going to be there. He said to one of the other cops, 'Hey, I've got it.' Then he said to me, 'Andrew, you got so many problems that this one's on us.' He put the license in his pocket and that was the last I ever heard about my fake identification.

"And then he asked me if I knew what this was all about. I told him I had no idea. He said, 'You're the last one we got. Your whole crew is in jail. This has something to do with your uncle down in Florida.' I knew he was talking about Nicky. And my marijuana partner thought that Nicky was my blood uncle. And who better to tell them about Joseph Conti than the guy who made up the documents for me? What Scanlon had said answered some of my questions.

"They had placed Charlotte in handcuffs too. Scanlon told me I had two options. I could keep my mouth shut and they'd arrest her along with me until they could find out if she had anything to do with the guns. Or I could be a man and take responsibility for what they'd found. If I did that, they'd just run a warrant check on her and turn her loose. I told them it was my place and anything they found was mine. I said let's leave civilians out of this. They ran their check, then released her.

"After they finished the search I was taken to a precinct on Coney Island Avenue in Brooklyn. That's where I first met a detective named Michael Callahan. He was working with the Joint Organized-Crime Task Force and was assigned to the Lucchese squad. Then they took me to another facility, where they said some people wanted to question me.

"While this was going on, Charlotte had called my mother, who in turn had contacted Mike Yannotti. He had her go to the office of his lawyer, a guy named Joe Muri. He told her that he'd see what he could do about getting me bailed out.

"I knew I was in a bad spot, but I wasn't sure exactly how bad. I was no doubt facing a lot of years behind bars from the legal system. And if I was willing to take it on the chin and do the time, I'd be protecting the very same guys who wanted me dead. I needed more time to think and try to figure out where things really stood for me. So when I talked with Callahan and an FBI agent named Vince Girard, I hinted that I might consider talking with them again. I didn't give them anything or promise them anything. I just kind of opened the door a crack for future reference.

"They explained to me that I'd be going through central booking and then to the Brooklyn House of Detention on the parole-violation charge. They'd arrest me again in a few days on federal charges. I told them I thought they were full of shit, that they didn't have anything on me. They kinda laughed at me. Like they were going to open my eyes real soon.

"The law had gotten a fugitive and a bunch of weapons off the streets. It was a good day for them. But in the long run, it was a pretty good day for me too."

18

Decision Time

Andrew had been in the Brooklyn House of Detention for a couple of days when he had visitors. Michael Callahan and another lawman wanted to see him. He turned down the visit. It wasn't that he'd changed his mind about possible co-operation. Rather, he thought the contact was too out in the open. Andrew didn't trust the guards at the facility and he knew how it would sound if the word got out that he was meeting with lawmen without an attorney present. And he'd already rejected the services of Joe Muri.

"I was initially held for only the parole violation," Andrew explains. "When Muri showed up at my arraignment, I told him there was nothing he could do for me. I wasn't going to get bail and had no need for a lawyer at that time. And when I did need one, I'd use Joseph Corozzo. That decision caused a lot of talk in organized-crime circles, because they couldn't figure out just what I was up to.

"A couple of mornings later, a correction officer woke me up around four-thirty and said I had to get ready for court. I told him I didn't have any court scheduled, that I was being held on a parole violation. He insisted. So I got dressed and they moved me to the holding pens where inmates waited for transportation to court or other appearances. Names were called out and guys left. It was now past court hours and I was the only one left in the cell. I complained to a correction officer that they'd just rousted me to bust my balls. There was no court for me.

"The officer said, 'Oh no. You're somethin' special. The marshals are comin' for you.' That's when I knew additional charges were about to be filed against me. They took me to Cadman Plaza in Brooklyn. I was met there by Michael Callahan, Vince Girard, and a couple of other guys. I was arrested, but only on a federal weapons charge at that time. That was because the serial number on the machine gun they found in my apartment had been filed off, making it a federal charge. After processing me, they wanted to talk.

"My choices were to tell them I didn't want to talk, would only speak with them if I had my lawyer with me, or talk with them right then. My mother had found a non-Mob lawyer for me and I already indicated to him that I was thinking about becoming a government witness. So I let it be known to them that I was open to a cooperation deal. I told them, though, that I was concerned about several things. I said that I wanted to get my lawyer involved and maybe something could be worked out. I said that any agreement we reached would have to include me doing any time as a federal prisoner.

"Because I was now in the federal system, I figured I'd be going to MDC [Metropolitan Detention Center] in Brooklyn where Nicky and Lenny were being held. But they had issued a separation order that we couldn't be housed in the same facility. In addition, I learned later that another guy housed at MDC, Timothy Lynskey, had been a friend of Robert Arena's and thought I was responsible for Robert's murder. For those reasons, I was sent to MCC [Metropolitan Correction Center] in Manhattan instead.

"When I arrived at MCC, I was assigned to the eleventh floor. Almost immediately, I was approached by Danny Marino, a capo in the Gambino family. A lot of other organized-crime guys were there from the various families. They treated me well, but I was in a very uncomfortable position. Although I was still on the fence, if they knew what I was thinking about doing, my treatment would have changed real quick.

"Meanwhile, the federal prosecutor's office was in contact with my lawyer. They told him they understood my situation and that I'd definitely been marked for death. That became crystal clear when I was arraigned before a female federal magistrate. When the subject came up, she said she'd consider setting bail. The prosecutor told the judge there was credible information that not only was the Gambino family plotting my murder, but other organized-crime families as well. If I went back onto the streets, it was unlikely I'd live to return to court.

"The magistrate said that because of the parole hold on me, I couldn't be released anyway. But if the parole situation got resolved, I'd have to decide whether or not I wanted to pursue bail, knowing the dire picture described by the prosecutor.

"The government continued to talk with my lawyer and they were playing hard ball. Their position was that they had me cold on the weapons charge and they were ready to file on me for drug dealing. My suspicions going back to the drug arrests in Vegas and the cops knowing about my fake identification when they arrested me were confirmed. My partner and the document guy were both government informants.

"And if I didn't cooperate, they planned to convict me and go for my throat at sentencing. They'd seek the maximum sentence on each count and ask that they run consecutively. Including the eight years I was facing for the parole violation, I was already looking at around forty years. But the kicker was they hadn't even mentioned the bank burglaries and robberies yet. And I didn't believe for a minute they didn't know about them. Adding those in, I'd be an old man when I got out of prison—if I got out at all.

"It was getting near crunch time. The feds wanted me on their side, but they wouldn't wait on me indefinitely. After cutting through all the bullshit, I had two choices. I could spend most of the rest of my life in prison to protect the man who wanted me dead and a bunch of guys who'd just as soon kill me as look at me. Or I could try to avoid that by becoming something I'd been taught to hate since I was a kid. I could switch sides and become a rat.

"I thought about it real hard. I honestly believe that if it was just a matter of doing the prison time, I'd have taken it on the chin. But what did I owe Nicky Corozzo? With Nicky, loyalty was a one-way street. He thought he was owed everyone's loyalty, that allegiance went up the ladder, but not down. At one time I thought Nicky walked on water. But I'd come to see him for what he really was. Over the last several months, I'd awoke to the fact that Nicky and the whole fuckin' life weren't what I'd thought they were when I was younger. So the answer to my own question was I didn't owe Nicky Corozzo a goddamn thing.

"Even realizing all that, it was still a hard decision—the hardest decision of my life. I'd been moved to the federal facility in Otisville, New York [located approximately 70 miles northwest of New York City]. I remember sitting on the bunk in my cell crying to myself, wondering if there was a truly right way to go.

"I have to say the most decisive factor during my internal deliberations was Michael Callahan. When we'd talked, he admitted he couldn't promise me anything. He said if I flipped, it wouldn't be an easy road. But when it was all over, my life would be my own. As far as I was concerned, during the past year he was the only one who told me the truth. His honesty impressed me and moved me along in the right direction. His truthfulness probably saved my life.

"After I made my decision, I told my lawyer that I wanted

to get serious about a deal. I mean, up until then, the government couldn't be totally sure how much value I'd have as a witness. And I didn't know exactly what they'd bring to the table. It was time to meet with the prosecutor and find out.

"Because of my parole thing, it was easy for me to leave the prison without creating suspicion. Whenever I was taken out, the other inmates assumed it had something to do with that. My first meeting was what's known as 'queen for a day.' That's when you can tell all you know and nothing you say can be used against you. The prosecutors can evaluate your credibility and how much of an asset you'd be.

"I must have made a good impression. After talking with me for about twenty minutes the prosecutor said I was a 'treasure trove' of information. She also said that what I was telling them would require a lot of investigation. There probably wouldn't be any visible action taken against Nicky or anyone else for about eighteen months. That said, she was ready to talk a deal. It boiled down to me promising to put it all out there as truthfully as I could. If I got caught lying or holding back, any promises the government made to me or any sentencing recommendations were out the window. And about the only real promise they made was to protect me and my family.

"After that I was transported from Otisville every so often to be debriefed. And the cover story, that my trips were mostly about my fight with the parole people, seemed to work like a charm. None of my fellow organized-crime inmates acted different toward me or gave me any reason to think they were suspicious of me.

"But working both sides of the fence is something I wouldn't recommend to anybody. I had to wonder how long it would be before someone got wise. I always worried about bumping into someone who knew me when I was coming in or out of one of those meetings. If I was seen somewhere I wasn't supposed to be, I knew the word would get around quick. And everybody knows that prison isn't a healthy place to be if they think you're a snitch.

"While I was in Otisville, my cellmate was a Genovese capo called Nicky the Blonde. And I met another Genovese guy named Tommy Barrett who was good friends with the bank-robbery crew I had worked with. Tommy was doing fourteen years for bank robbery himself.

"After we became friends, I told Tommy that I was fighting a battle to get bail set in my parole case. If I could do that, I had a shot at bail on the federal charge too. With some luck, I could possibly end up back out on the street.

"Tommy said that because I'd robbed with his friends, he knew I was trustworthy. He said he had a connection with the Brinks company who'd be able to give us a money truck. If I got out, he wanted to use me to get that message to Joe Miraglia, Tommy Scuderi, and Sal DeMeo. They'd take down the truck and he could make a score while sittin' in prison.

"I hadn't been lookin' for that information. It just kinda fell into my lap. At my next debriefing, I told them about it.

"The government wanted to have me out on bail too. Not just for the Brinks deal, though. They figured I'd be able to get close to Mike Yannotti and wear a wire on him.

"But when I finally had my parole hearing, the judge said no way was she going to let me out. She said that I shot people for a living and was way too dangerous. She wouldn't have any part in releasing me back into society. The federal prosecutor's recommendation had absolutely no effect on her. She gave me the maximum sentence she could on the parole violation—eight years. And I believe her decision to throw the book at me saved my life.

"Nicky wanted me dead. He thought I was holding back money from him. He also thought I was being a smartass by helping put money into the pockets of guys from other families. But I think his biggest thing against me was that I was the only person who could tie him and Mike Yannotti to

Robert Arena's murder. They knew it and I knew it. There was no doubt in my mind that if they got the opportunity, they'd kill me. They'd have felt they had no choice. If I went back on the street, I was a dead man, wire or no wire.

"Don't get me wrong. If it worked out that way, I'd have fought for my life. But there's no way you can win a fight with the family boss. Another crewmate or guys from another family, maybe you got a chance. But not when you're up against the boss. Then there's no winning, no chance for survival. Maybe I'd have gone out in a blaze of glory and taken Mike or some others with me. But after all was said and done, I'd have ended up being a ten-minute conversation in a bar and I didn't want that. Under the situation I was in, staying behind bars was my best chance—my only chance—to stay alive."

● ● ●

Andrew continued to play his dangerous game: maintaining his appearance of being just another gangster in trouble with the law in the eyes of his fellow inmates, while secretly greasing the wheels of justice during his clandestine meetings with government prosecutors. He was frequently moved between Otisville and various courthouses. Sometimes he spent a night or two housed at the MCC. A conversation he had with a Lucchese capo during one such stay in late 1997 is etched in his mind.

"One night around Christmas we were sitting in a cell talking. He said, 'Look at us. We're sittin' here in jail like two idiots. Our friends are out drinkin' and laughin' and havin' a good time. But they don't realize that their lives are on oxygen tanks too.'

"Then he pointed out the window toward the courthouse and said, 'Do you see that building across the street with the offices all lit up? They're working over there around the clock to put you, me, and our friends away forever. Our friends go to sleep, but those guys never do. They're always out there buildin' their cases. So while our friends are celebratin' Christmas, right in one of those rooms somebody's signing their indictments. The government has too much money and too many people. We can never win this war.'

"He was right and me and him knew it. But there were a lot of guys still in the life that didn't."

19

Tremors

In 1998, Andrew came to realize that his decision to become a government witness was a bed of thorns, just as Michael Callahan had predicted. Although he was comfortable with providing information against Nicky Corozzo, Mike Yannotti, and others, he would also be required to share what he knew about those he considered to be friends, such as the bank-robbery crew. And even his mother wasn't completely supportive.

He also knew that when his information bore fruit and indictments and arrests became public, his role would be exposed. That would likely be followed by having to face his former associates in a courtroom. This was not a pleasant prospect. But the alternative was worse. So, in spite of those drawbacks, Andrew honored his agreement with the government.

Besides, as Andrew reflected on his life and on organized crime in general during his sessions with prosecutors, he experienced a true appreciation for how that life had affected him, his family, friends, enemies, and victims. When looking at the total picture, he was stunned by the havoc he and his associates had wreaked. Many people had been hurt who didn't deserve to be hurt. Several were dead who didn't have to die. His decision to cooperate became more than just a means of survival for him. It also presented an opportunity to atone for his own actions and perhaps help him to move on in a positive direction after his deal with the government had been fulfilled.

"Living up to my end of the bargain with the government wasn't always easy," Andrew recalls, "especially at the beginning, before I came to grips with what a bad person I'd been. But during my many hours talking with prosecutors, I had to relive my life all the way back to my teens. Crime by crime, I had to tell them what I'd done, who with, and why. Who I'd tried to kill and who I'd wanted to kill. The robberies, larcenies, frauds, drug deals—on and on. And I had to tell them about things I hadn't done personally and had only heard about.

"As I put it all out there, I was shocked by my own admissions. The things I'd done hadn't seemed so bad when I was doin' them; they'd seemed natural to me. I was a tough guy and a gangster and those things were what guys like me did. And I'd done them without givin' it a second thought. But looking back at them in their totality, it was hard to believe I was talking about myself. The picture I painted was that all my adult life, I'd looked for ways to take advantage of somebody from the time I got up until I went to bed. I tried to tell myself that I really hadn't been that bad. But the evidence was overwhelming. I was thirty-two years old and I'd been a real bastard for half of that time.

"And when I was being honest with myself, I couldn't even blame it on my environment. It contributed, sure. But I knew right from wrong. Nicky didn't hold a gun to my head and tell me to commit crimes for him. It was my reputation as a thief and tough kid that brought me to his attention. The choices I'd made were mine. I couldn't find anyone else to blame.

"But those realizations about myself and organized crime occurred over time. My toughest obstacles at first were having to give up my friends along with my enemies and convincing my mother that I had made the right decision.

"Unfortunately, a government witness doesn't get to pick who or what he'll talk about. The prosecutors had made it very clear that they wouldn't accept anything from me but total honesty. Nothing was off the table—not my own crimes or those that I committed with others. That meant I had to throw my buddies from the bank-robbery crew under the bus along with everybody else. That was a real hard thing to do at the beginning. Later, I came to accept the fact that we were all part of the life. And the way the game is played, it's the bottom line that counts in the end. If Nicky had kept the pressure on them about how much we actually made in that New Jersey bank robbery and some other scores, they'd have eventually given me up. That's the way it works.

"My mother wasn't upset about the cooperation aspect of my deal. She was concerned about the long-term effects. The way she looked at it, some of the high-profile guys who turned government witness, guys like Sammy the Bull, had lots of money stashed when they flipped. They could start over again a lot easier than I'd be able to. She worried that they'd stick me in some Godforsaken place with no money and no way to establish myself. But after a while, she realized that there wasn't really any other option for me and she knew it was the right move.

"My nervousness came from the lack of knowing exactly what kind of sentence I was going to get when I had to face a judge and pay for all the crimes I was admitting to. The prosecutor's promise of a sentencing recommendation didn't tell me a hell of a lot. I knew the New Jersey bank job could carry a long prison term all by itself. And a felon in possession of a weapon was serious as well. I could still end up in prison until I was an old man. I didn't think that would happen. But the uncertainty was there."

• • •

For the next several months, Andrew continued his routine: shuttled among Otisville, MCC, and various courthouses. Although he would eventually enter the first phase of the federal Witness Protection Program—the phase for incarcerated witnesses—for the time being he remained in general population.

"In prison, like on the streets, you run into some guys you like and some you don't. One of those I met was Theodore Persico, my friend Teddy Persico's father. I liked him, but he was a little eccentric. We met in Otisville and after the first twenty minutes of conversation, I surmised that he was a pretty thrifty guy. In fact, I figured he probably still had the first nickel he ever made in organized crime. For example, New York State charged nickel deposits on their soda cans. He went around the prison and collected the cans from the trash barrels and turned them in for the deposit. Considering that Theodore was a boss, money certainly wasn't an issue for him. Like I said, he was a nice guy, but a bit odd."

Andrew really shouldn't have been surprised that the elder Persico wasn't a free spender. If like-father-like-son is any indication, Andrew's dealings with Danny Persico, Theodore's son, should have tipped him off.

"Danny, me, and some of our associates met for dinners and lunches multiple time per week. And during these outings, Danny was known for always leaving others with the tab. During our friendship, it became a long-running joke. I really liked Danny and it was all in good fun.

"One day me, Tommy Dono, and Benny Geritano returned the favor by playing a trick on Danny that he wouldn't forget. It was an afternoon and we were hanging around a friend's social club in Bensonhurst. There were about ten of us and we were gettin' a little hungry, so we went to this neighborhood restaurant that was owned by a friend of ours. It was also one of Danny's favorite spots. So I called Danny and told him he could meet us there when he was through with his business in Manhattan.

"Our timing was perfect. We knew we'd be long gone before Danny got there. After ordering like kings, with six bottles of wine and entrées, I went downstairs and put the plan into place. I used the pay phone to call the restaurant upstairs. Doing my best impersonation of Danny's squeaky voice, I asked to speak with the owner.

"I said, 'It's cousin Danny. Are Andrew and the boys there? Good. Listen to me. Today is Tommy's birthday. I'm supposed to be there, but I can't make it. So make sure I get the bill. Don't charge anyone and I'll stop by in a few hours and pay the tab.'

"I hung up the phone and went back upstairs. The owner stopped at our table a couple of minutes later. He said Danny had called and said our meals and all the trimmings—nearly a thousand dollars worth—were on him. There was a moment of silence as we all looked at each other and then burst out laughing.

"When we left the restaurant, we went down the street to a bar we frequented. Danny was dating a girl who worked there and we knew he'd show up after he stopped at the restaurant. Within an hour, Danny came flyin' through the door. His face was beet red and he was waving the bill in the air. He yelled across the room, 'Andrew, are you on fuckin' medication?'

"We were all laughing so hard we could hardly breathe. We bought Danny a drink. In a couple of minutes he'd calmed down and was laughing with us. He knew he had it coming."

● ● ●

During his confinement, Andrew met some other interesting organized-crime figures and gained valuable insights into the mentality of many of the bosses. The results were both disappointing and beneficial.

He met Andrew Russo at MCC. He'd been a Colombo boss at one time and in the streets his whole life. Still, he came across as intelligent and well-read. He had a wide range of interests and could carry on a conversation on almost any subject. Andrew's time spent with Russo during their incarceration was definitely a learning experience.

Russo's son Jo Jo was there too, on a conviction from the Colombo war. Jo Jo passed away not long ago. Andrew doesn't relish speaking ill of the dead, but he says Jo Jo wasn't like his father. He was more like a baby. Every day he whined about his conviction.

"Those guys sat in MCC for seven years fightin' and appealin' their cases. I couldn't believe they didn't want to go to Otisville so they could at least get some fresh air. But they didn't. They stayed at MCC the whole time.

"It's funny that you hear a lot about some of these guys, who are kinda like legends when they're on the streets. But when you see them behind bars, you find out they're human beings like the rest of us. They put their pants on like the rest of us and they've got their own strengths and weaknesses. That can be a letdown, because sometimes their street personalities aren't as colorful when you meet them in person behind bars.

"I learned a lot about some of those guys I'd thought were larger than life while I was locked up with them. What I saw contributed to my changing attitude about organized crime and the people in it. Most of what I'd thought it was didn't really exist. The camaraderie, the idea that it was one big family where everybody took care of each other, was all bullshit. During my last several months on the streets, I'd learned that true friends were few and far between. And that guys like Nicky Corozzo didn't give a fuck about anybody but themselves. When they could use you to make them rich and take care of their dirty work for them, you were okay. But if you stopped producing or got so good at your job that you became a threat, you became expendable. And make no mistake, we were all expendable.

"People think that those of us who become government witnesses turned against the bosses. The reality is the bosses turned against us. The guys in middle management and on the streets have to follow certain protocols. But not the bosses. They change the rules or make new ones to suit their own situations. They take from their underlings until there's nothing left. Then they put them in no-win situations where they either have to pay with their life or give up their life. And I'll tell you something, anybody who doesn't believe that and decides to get into the life is in for a rude fuckin' awakening.

"So those days gave me a front-row seat into the mindset of the big shots as they planned their strategy on how they'd defend themselves in court. I've heard it said that watching sausage being made isn't a pretty sight. For me, seeing and hearing what was going on was the organized-crime version of making sausage. Those guys had no loyalty to anybody. The so-called principles that I once thought everybody, even the bosses, abided by were laid bare as lies. As those scenarios unfolded, on the one hand I felt like a real sucker. I'd bought into that crap hook, line, and sinker. On the other hand, it made me feel better about what I was doing. The whole Mafia thing in my day was built on lies and misconceptions. These guys didn't feel the least bit guilty about what they'd done or were prepared to do. I was beginning to have no regrets either."

● ● ●

Andrew longed to see his son. But Dina wouldn't allow it,

citing the fact that because he was involved in a serious relationship with Charlotte, visitation wouldn't be appropriate. That didn't sit very well with him.

"Dina was what I call a sauce maker. And I don't mean in the kitchen. She seemed to cause trouble for me at every turn. She didn't want to live with me, but didn't want anybody else to have me either. I think she was relishing the fact that I was in prison and hoped that I'd need her somewhere down the line. I refused to kiss her ass and she used my son as leverage against me. So I didn't see him at all for two years—while I was on the run and while I was in Otisville and MCC.

● ● ●

In the late summer of 1998, Andrew went to court and admitted his part in the 1996 New Jersey bank robbery. Shortly after that, prosecutors informed him that the cases he had provided information on were moving forward and indictments would be forthcoming in the near future. He knew when that happened, the cat would be partially out of the bag. There would be suspicion at the least; eventually, the whole story would get out.

"The first case was going to be against the bank-robbery crew," Andrew said. "That made me kind of sad. But the choice wasn't mine. And knowing they'd have had no choice but to give me up to Nicky somewhere down the line made it a little easier.

"I appeared before Judge Charles P. Sifton on September third for sentencing on the bank-robbery plea. It was kind of a surreal experience. None of the cases I was helping with had been announced yet, so he'd have to take the prosecutor's word about how helpful I was being. If he wasn't convinced, he could have given me thirty years. That made me pretty nervous and I had butterflies when I stood before him. As he talked, he said he wondered how many generations organized crime would ruin. And then he started to cry. The first thing I thought was that he was going to use me as an example that society had to get tough on crime.

"But he didn't. He said he'd been told the extent of my cooperation and sentenced me to forty-eight months. He stated that he was uncomfortable giving me that much time and he ordered that his sentence run concurrent with the eight years I'd been given for the parole violation. He added that if I could rectify my parole situation, he'd consider bringing me back to further reduce the sentence he'd just handed down.

"Under the circumstances, the news couldn't have been any better. The almost twenty months I'd been locked up counted toward his sentence. Adding in my good-time allowance, my federal sentence timed out on November seventh, 2000.

"Just days after the sentencing, a correction officer got me up around four-thirty in the morning and told me I was being moved to the Hole. Nicky the Blonde was my cellmate and he was concerned that the move was disciplinary. But I knew it was the first move in getting to the Witness Protection unit. Later that same day, the first arrests in the bank-robbery case came down: Paul Mazzarese, Tommy Scuderi, and Joe Miraglia. Sal DeMeo made an agreement to turn himself in, but went on the lam instead. The word quickly circulated in the newspapers and on the streets.

"Right after that, correction officers who knew me from the compound would stop by my cell and ask what was going on. I knew better than to tell them anything, because any one of them could have been playing both sides of the fence.

"One of the officers I knew a little better than the others told me that trouble was breaking out in the compound over me. Some inmates said I'd sold out and others said that would never happen. Speculation about me was running rampant. As tempers flared, organized-crime guys were getting into fist fights among themselves. I'm sure there were a lot of people, including Nicky, hoping my defenders were right. If they weren't and I'd actually flipped, they knew there was trouble ahead."

The rumblings about Andrew's possible cooperation with the government caused shock waves both inside and outside of the prison. Unfortunately, he had to stay in the Hole until he was formally accepted into the federal Witness Protection Program.

WITNESS PROTECTION—
HISTORY AND PROCESS

The federal Witness Protection Program (WPP) was implemented in 1970 to protect crucial government witnesses whose prospective testimony put them in immediate danger. Since its inception, more than 7,500 witnesses and 9,500 witness family members have entered the program and have been protected, relocated, and given new identities. It is operated by the U.S. Marshals Service.

The cost of operating the WPP is substantial. The total cost of bringing one witness and his immediate family into the program in 1997 was approximately $150,000. The operating budget for the program in fiscal year 1996 was $46.3 million. The following year it grew to $61.8 million.

A 1997 article about the WPP by Ridson N. Slate states the case for such expenditures: "U.S. Attorneys throughout the nation state that the program is the most valuable tool that they have in fighting organized crime and major criminal activity. Over 100 mobsters are purported to be participants in the WPP. For example, the testimony of alleged protected witness Salvatore Gravano, who was reportedly involved in nineteen murders and actually acknowledged pulling the trigger in one hit, proved instrumental in sending mob boss John Gotti to prison for life. In addition, terrorists, drug traffickers, members of motorcycle and prison gangs, and other major criminals have been adversely affected by the testimony of protected witnesses."

The same article further states that in all the cases involving protected-witness testimony since the program's inception, the government has reportedly realized a conviction rate of 89%—an impressive statistic that makes clear that familiarity on the part of witnesses often goes beyond casual observations and includes involvement in the criminal enterprise. Ninety-seven percent of witnesses entering the program have had criminal records and been deeply involved in some type of criminal activity. And somewhat surprisingly, according to the United States Marshals Service, the recidivism rate for witnesses with prior criminal histories who entered the program and were later arrested and charged with crimes is less than 23%. This recidivism percentage among program participants is less than half the rate of those released from the nation's prisons.

The process for admission into the WPP isn't automatic and involves input from several sources. However, final determinations are made by the U.S. Attorney General. Typically, applications for witness protection are submitted by various United States Attorneys and Organized Crime Strike Forces across the country. In addition to the sponsoring attorney's application, the case agent from the investigative agency provides a threat assessment through his federal headquarters for review. In rendering its decision, the Attorney General takes into consideration information from the United States Attorney, the investigative agency, and the United States Marshals Service. The relevant information includes the importance of the testimony, the possibility of obtaining the desired testimony from someone else, a psychological evaluation of the prospective witness to determine the risk to the community to which the witness will be relocated, and a recommendation by the Marshals Service assessing the suitability of the witness for the program.

Prisoner witnesses can also apply for protected testimony. The Bureau of Prisons is responsible for protection of prisoner witnesses while incarcerated. The Marshals Service provides secure transportation to and from court and safe testimony. Provided sponsorship is available, prisoner witnesses can also apply for protection upon release from prison.

A federal investigation and consideration of the likelihood of the prospective witness' death are essential elements in the assessment of applications for the WPP. Those who are accepted into the program cease to exist under their old names. A check for old records would show that the entrant never existed prior to his or her new identity. Participants may choose their new name as long as it's ethnically compatible and is not a previously used or a family name. New documentation includes a driver's license, Social Security card, birth certificate, and diplomas to the level of education that one has actually attained.

Entrants into the WPP undergo an initiation and introduction to the program at a safe site and orientation center situated in metropolitan Washington, D.C. The location is highly secret and secure, bearing no address. In addition to name changes and new documentation, participants are familiarized with information regarding the area from which they supposedly originate. Though contacts back home are discouraged, participants can initiate, but not receive, calls and can keep in touch through secure mail-forwarding channels. Discretionary money is available for rent, furniture, clothes, automobiles, and so forth. Finally, in a signed Memorandum of Understanding, the responsibilities of participants and the Marshals Service are defined.

According to the Marshals Service, "In both criminal and civil matters involving protected witnesses, the Marshals Service cooperates fully with local law enforcement and court authorities in bringing witnesses to justice or in having them fulfill their legal responsibilities."

However, in his article, Mr. Slate takes issue with that statement, writing: "As an analysis of the history of the WPP shows, along with litigation, and subsequent hearings, it is questionable whether such cooperation has always occurred. The witness protection statutes contemplated only the protection of witnesses and their families—not protection of the public from the witness. This Machiavellian approach of putting governmental interests first has served to taint the origins and development of the WPP."

● ● ●

The victim of a glitch, Andrew remained in the Hole for four months. The prosecutors and agents he was working with thought he had already been moved. While they were preparing to visit him in his new home, they found he was still in Otisville. Shortly after that, he was given and passed a polygraph exam and was finally ready to enter the first phase of the WPP on December 16, 1998. It was a move he welcomed.

"Those four months in the Hole were pretty stressful for me," Andrew remembers. "By the time they transferred me, I'd lost ten or fifteen pounds and hadn't had a haircut in months and seldom shaved. I must have looked like somebody who'd been stranded on a deserted island for a while. I was pretty aggravated with the way things had gone. It was the kind of therapy I didn't need. But I finally was formally accepted.

"Entering the Program meant moving to a special housing unit with other inmates like yourself. These are usually smaller settings placed in strategic locations across the United States. I have too much respect for the marshals to name any of the locations. All I'll say is that they're federally run and the officers who work in those facilities are specially trained.

"I was with guys from other organized-crime families throughout the country, motorcycle gangs, drug gangs—just about anybody who had been engaged in major gang or organized-crime activity. It was a real learning experience.

"Being in a small setting, I got to meet and know everybody very quickly. And I found out right away that some of those guys weren't satisfied to just do their time. They were always looking to get somebody else in trouble. They figured that by ratting on their fellow inmates, they could get a better deal for themselves and get some time shaved off their sentence. They spent their time scheming and plotting. It was a shame, because we were all in the same boat, fighting the same war. But that's the way it was. Because of that, I limited the number of people I spent time with to a couple of guys I trusted.

"For the rest of that year and into the next, I spent a lot of time with the prosecutors putting other cases together. One of them involved the Colombo drug-dealing operation. Another was against Wild Bill Cutolo in a shylocking and racketeering case, other drug cases, and the double homicide case involving the death of my friend Robert Arena.

"And some of the guys on the streets were trying to get messages to me through my family that I should stop cooperating, because I was hurting some good solid people. That was all a bunch of bullshit. These were some of the same people who wanted me dead before I flipped. And then they had the fuckin' balls to say I should protect them. Those bastards had no shame."

● ● ●

Andrew headed into 1999 with renewed dedication to his task. Progress was being made in the criminal cases he was helping put together. Unfortunately, another former friend wouldn't make it through the year.

20

1999

Two of the three major events for Andrew in 1999 involved the Colombo family. The third concerned the bank-robbery crew. First on the agenda was the case he was helping the FBI build against four Colombo drug dealers.

Anticipating having to testify at trial against the Colombo men, it came as a pleasant surprise to Andrew when the four defendants made deals with prosecutors and entered guilty pleas. He and the other witnesses were off the hook. Although the convictions hadn't been rendered by a jury, the pleas were a testament to the strength of the government's case, which was based partly on the information he provided.

On the heels of that news, Andrew learned that the bank-robbery crew members were also negotiating pleas. That included Sal DeMeo, who was in custody after an appearance on "America's Most Wanted."

While these developments relieved a certain amount of Andrew's stress, they didn't remove it all. He was still confined with 60 other men, all of whom were government witnesses. And many of them were always looking for an opportunity to come up with incriminating information against someone that they could swap to better their own situations. The small space allotted for the witness units limited recreational activities compared to a regular prison. But the lack of a yard large enough to play football or handball was somewhat made up for by one-man cells and television sets.

No matter the accommodations, nothing could make the inmates stop worrying about the safety of their loved ones. Would the friends of a gangster imprisoned on his testimony seek revenge by harming someone the witness held dear?

On the other side of the coin were the inmates whose families had turned on them over their decision to cooperate with the government. They received no support at all from their disgruntled kin. So everyone incarcerated in that facility had his own reason for anxiety.

For Andrew, the seemingly endless hours of debriefing by FBI agents and prosecutors seeking every detail of his involvement in or knowledge of specific crimes was emotionally draining. Reflecting back on it now, he finds that was probably the most insecure period of his life. Nothing felt certain. He was always afraid of what the future held, always wondering how many cases he'd be called to testify at after the agents and lawyers had wrung every bit of information out of him.

What would it be like when he got out of prison and had to start fresh as a brand new person who had never before existed? Andrew DiDonato, the career tough guy and criminal, would be gone. Who would replace him?

And then there was his son, whom he hadn't seen in two years. It didn't appear that Dina was doing anything to help him salvage a relationship with the boy. That issue was never far from his thoughts. He feared losing his son to the very life he'd just walked away from. Even today, he gets nauseous when he remembers the feelings of sadness and helplessness he experienced at that time.

Those feelings were compounded in late May when news from the organized-crime world hit the witness unit like a bolt of lightning. And it struck Andrew particularly hard: Colombo family underboss Wild Bill Cutolo had gone missing. In Andrew's former life, that meant the man was either on the run or dead. And there was no reason to believe that Wild Bill was on the run.

"A lot of things went through my mind," Andrew remembers. "I thought about my old friend Billy Junior and what he must be going through. And I thought about Wild Bill. Even though we'd had our differences, I'd always respected him. I really felt bad when I remembered that last time I'd seen him on the street corner with Danny Cataia. I was pissed off that day and said things to Wild Bill I shouldn't have. But I said what I said and there was no way to take it back.

"The theory around Wild Bill's disappearance was that it was a repercussion from the Colombo war. Wild Bill had backed the Vic Orena faction of the family in trying to forcibly take control away from Carmine Persico. Orena lost and Persico stayed in power. It figured that Wild Bill's disappearance was related to challenging Persico and coming out on the losing side.

"Looking at it from the outside, it seemed that Carmine probably saw Wild Bill as a threat. He was a very powerful boss with a crew and financial backing. He had a lot influence with the other crime families and Carmine probably thought he might make another try to take over.

"If Wild Bill was dead, I wondered what chance Billy Junior had to stay alive, if any. In the life, if you decide to kill somebody, it's always advisable to take out anybody who might want to seek revenge. And there was no doubt in my mind that if Billy Junior knew or found out who made his father vanish, he'd want retribution. So I didn't see much chance of him staying alive for very long.

"Thank God I was wrong."

WILD BILL CUTOLO

The disappearance and presumed death of Wild Bill caused Andrew to regret his words during their last heated encounter. And his concern for the safety of his friend Billy Jr. made it a double blow. But certainly the man suffering the most over Wild Bill's loss was Billy Jr. himself. In the following paragraphs, Billy talks about his father, the day he went missing, and the ensuing years.

"My name is William P. Cutolo, Junior. I've also been known as Billy, Junior, Bones, and Rat. That latter name is one I despise.

"My father was William P. Cutolo. By some he was called Wild Bill or Billy Fingers. And the latter name he despised. He was the number-two guy in the Colombo crime family out of Brooklyn, New York. For those who don't know the details of such a despicable life—Mafia, Mob, organized crime—the second slot meant he was the 'Underboss' of the family. He was second in command to Carmine 'The Snake' Persico, who occupied the number-one slot.

"My father was a man larger than life. He was an extremely smart man and had the brains to be whatever in life he wanted to be. He dressed in custom-made suits and hand-painted ties. Seeing him on the street in the morning and not knowing any better, the average person would have thought he was just some white-collar guy on the way to his job in New York City.

"One of the reasons for his success was that he was a man of his word and the other four crime families in New York knew it. He was a guy who demanded respect and it came easy to him.

"My father had survived numerous attempts on his life throughout his many years on the streets. And he lived through a gangland civil war between two factions of the Colombo family in which over a dozen men were killed and numerous others went to jail with lengthy prison terms. He almost seemed invincible.

"But that all changed on May twenty-sixth, nineteen-ninety-nine. On the fateful day, he was called to a high-level meeting with the boss of the family and the number-three guy in the chain of command, the consigliere. He never returned.

"On that day, a close friend of my father's and I were doing our usual Wednesday routine of haircuts, manicures, and then off to our social club in Brooklyn. When my father didn't arrive there, I immediately started asking who may have seen him. I received nothing but, 'No, Bill, we haven't seen him.'

"I tried to think of a legitimate reason for him to not be around. Maybe he was with someone and he couldn't get back to me. Or if he was at a high-level meeting [where only high-ranking members of organized crime were present], all beepers and cell phones had to be checked at the door, so to speak—anything that could be considered a listening device had to be out of the room. Even so, whenever I paged him and added a 'nine-eleven' after the phone number, he knew it was an emergency and always got back to me within minutes. But not that day.

"As the night grew on, I sat and played cards with friends, and an unusual question was whispered in my ear.

"'Have you spoken to your Pop today?' That's when it really hit me. That's when I knew he wasn't coming back. I bided my time the rest of that night and showed little reaction. But the next morning, I set things into action that allowed me to be alive today to tell the story.

"I knew that my father had good rapport with the other families. I did my homework and by the morning after, I knew who was responsible for my father's disappearance and murder, but I didn't know exactly why they wanted him dead. My father and thirteen others had been charged with multiple crimes after the so-called Colombo war. They were locked up for thirteen months before being acquitted on all charges. All was said to have been forgiven within the family after he was released from jail. But I found out that wasn't true. And that's what provided the motive and set the wheels in motion leading to my father's murder.

"My dad called a spade a spade. If he thought a guy was a rat, including a boss, he didn't bite his tongue about it. He told it like it was. Being outspoken doesn't set well with some people. And the powers that be were afraid of his power and his strong support. He was a true tough guy and whatever he touched turned to gold. He was the true meaning of an 'earner' in the life. And that in itself can get you killed. Jealousy and envy have led to a lot of deaths in the world of organized crime.

"As the next couple of days passed, all his crew came to me one at a time to express their sympathy for my loss. Not too long after, just days in fact, a guy who was supposed to be my father's best friend came to my mother's home in Staten Island and asked her where my father kept his financial ledgers and his stash of money. He even tapped on walls and floors thinking the money was hidden behind or under them. He came up empty. I have to say it was a bittersweet moment seeing the look on his face when I told him there was no ledger or money. It was priceless.

"He didn't know it, but my mother had been told by my father years earlier that if anything ever happened to him, she was to give them [his criminal associates] nothing. That's exactly what we did—gave them nothing. It was a victory, but it didn't bring my father home or his killers to justice.

"I love my family. But let's face it, when it came to my father's disappearance, what were they gonna do about it? They didn't know what to do. None of them did. They were scared. They were in shock. They weren't in the streets every day like me. I wanted to save them. I wanted to be the one that brought my father home. Home to have a proper burial like he and our family deserved. But most of all for him. I mean dogs, cats, even birds all get buried by their loved ones. Granted they're pets, but I hope you get my point. I knew I was the only person in a position to do anything. My knowledge of the players and how the game is played gave me the means to catch the girls [a derogatory reference regarding the manhood of the killers] responsible for my father's death. So I vowed I would not rest until he was found.

"Literally two days later, I received a visit at my father's home from two law-enforcement officials. I wasn't under any obligation to report my father's disappearance to the FBI or the police, so I ignored them at first. They left business cards from both the FBI and the NYPD.

"But after a while, I reached out to a detective and an agent I knew. I'd been in the company of the detective before, even though we were on opposite sides. I'd also gotten to know the agent over the years and he was a straight shooter. They knew my father was missing and presumed he was dead. They offered their condolences and warned me about the possible repercussions if I took vengeance on my own. After that they asked me, 'Do you want to know what happened to your father? Would you like to aid in the investigation?'

"Up until then, my only friend was a silent one. It was a friend without a conscience. It held fifteen in a clip and one in the chamber. And I wanted the blood of the men who killed my father so bad. I wanted their families to feel the pain of losing a father, a grandfather, and a husband like we had to endure. For me, killing those responsible would have been easy. Refraining from killing them would be much harder. But I forced myself to think. My father had warned me that if you kill one, two come at you. You put two down and four are coming, and so on. I knew he was right. And I had a wife and a son of my own to worry about. So I decided to break the cycle. To save spilling their blood and hit them another way.

"And so I did. In the next few seconds, my whole life changed. I became a member of the guys in the white hats and was no longer an outlaw in black. Now my anger was channeled and fueled with fire. I hit them and hit them hard. For almost two years, I secretly aided in the investigation. I caused havoc amongst the hierarchy of the Colombo family.

"The men I knew were responsible for my father sent for me on numerous occasions and I ignored them. When they sent two morons to threaten me if I didn't go where they wanted to take me, I introduced them to my silent friend and his sixteen buddies. They quickly left, saying only, 'Okay, Billy. We brought you the message.' I told them not to come back unless they thought they could carry me out. That if they were really my friends, they wouldn't have come with the message they did.

"At that point, I had no time in my schedule for pussies like them. I considered myself a man's man as I'd been taught by my father. At one time, nobody had more respect for the life than I did. But that went away with my father. Now my only loyalty was to him and the promise I'd made to him.

"Each time I went out to get information for the investigation, it was a rush and the more cocky I got. I was daring them to do something to me. But it never came. Call it what you will, but I say my father was looking down on me and kept me safe. He'd fed me the paranoia that still lives in me today. He always told me, 'Paranoia is good. It keeps you sharp.' It worked for me. My mind remained keen and I stayed alive.

"Right to this day, some people are still mad at me for not going out with guns blazing. That doesn't bother me. I'd do it all over again if I had to. My only regret is that I couldn't tell my family what I was doing. I wanted to, but I was warned that it wouldn't be a good idea. So I had to keep them in the dark.

"I delivered for the law, too. Even without finding his body, after eight years the government charged and convicted two men for my father's murder. So my cooperation and a few years in Witness Protection paid off.

"And then in early October of 2008, nine years after he went missing, I was out eating at Emeril's restaurant when the news came across the AP wire. It wasn't yet confirmed, but the authorities were pretty sure they'd found the location of my father's remains. I rushed out to get to a computer to monitor the news sites. I had mixed emotions. Was it really going to be over after all those years?

"It was. An examination confirmed that the remains were his. Many times I'd given up on God and law enforcement bringing that closure. Because one of the men convicted for the murder was an avid sailor, I figured they might have dumped his body at sea. So my confidence in anybody ever finding him was slim to none.

"My father's burial site was on Long Island in a small town called Farmingdale. The morons that killed him were too lazy to get rid of the body. They buried him fifteen minutes from the private home of the family's new street boss. He was wrapped neatly in a tarp with a single gunshot wound to the back of his head. The scars on his right arm and dental records confirmed that the corpse was indeed my father. My family was relieved at that moment and they were able to move on. But I wasn't. I'm still not the same person I was before my father's murder and I never will be.

"The difference between me and other people involved in my father's life is that I finished what I started. I had the means to an end. I never had to actually take the stand against his killers. However, I did get to sit in the courtroom about fifteen feet from two of them. I sneered at them and they wouldn't look at me. There wasn't even a jury present and they were afraid to look at me. I remember saying to them before the judge came in and only the lawyers were present, 'What's the matter, you ain't got nothin' to say? You two bastards don't even have the balls to look me in the eye?'

"When court was over, the judge thanked me for all my work and dedication. And most importantly for not falling through the cracks of society. On my way out of the court-room, I made sure I waved to the morons.

"Today I'm active in the wars against organized crime and domestic violence. And I try to help solve cold cases whenever I can. I think that's important, because if we all walked around with our heads in the sand, nobody's disappearance would ever get solved. I love being an activist in this crazy world. I love knowing that I can and do make a difference. I instill that idea in my children and I am greatly rewarded for that each day when I open my eyes and put both feet on the floor. I know that's what my father would have wanted. I still miss him so. And I speak with him daily in my thoughts and prayers.

"Looking back on it, I know I could have hurt a lot of other guys, but I didn't. Many of my father's crew and associates loved him and I knew who they were. Anybody that got caught in the crosshairs of my cooperation with the law has only himself to blame. If they want to know why they're in jail, they only have to look in the mirror. I was taught at a young age that any moron can hurt someone. But it takes a man to extend his hand and help that person back up. And that's the way I see myself today.

"Closure is a very fickle word. It has different meanings to other families and individuals. It doesn't bring a loved one back. But it puts your heart and mind at ease knowing that the person you cared so much for has been laid to rest. Knowing my father's murderers will die in prison helps, too. It doesn't take away the hurt, though. I wish I could say it did for me, but that would be a lie. The pain will always be there.

"I do have to say that after all the years we went without knowing for sure where he was, I now take nothing for granted. I stop and smell the roses and appreciate human life for all that it is. I'm happy with the choices I made then. I wasn't in any legal trouble and I wasn't facing jail time. I did what I did because I was tired of the life and it was the right thing to do. I want to be remembered for that.

"Today I'm the boss of a family. It's a family that consists of my wife and children. And they don't call me capo or the don. In my family, they call me Dad."

● ● ●

Another of Andrew's former associates was involved in some action in 1999. That December, electronics expert and bank robber Sal "Fat Sal" Mangiavillano paid a visit to Phoenix, Arizona. His mission: Kill super-rat Sammy "the Bull" Gravano, John Gotti Senior's former lieutenant.

The story came to light in June 2002, when Sal was still locked up on a 2001 arrest for bank-burglary charges. He contacted the FBI and told them that he had information that could implicate Peter Gotti, John Gotti Senior's brother and the current Gambino family boss, in a murder plot. Were the feds interested in talking deal?

They were. And what Sal had to say hadn't been heard by government ears before: that Peter Gotti had sanctioned a hit on the despised gangster-turned-snitch Sammy Gravano, the man who put Gotti Senior behind bars.

Mangiavillano told agents that on Peter Gotti's orders, he and former Gravano crew member Thomas "Huck" Carbonaro headed for Phoenix in December 1999 to kill the traitorous Gravano. Driving Sal's 1992 Mercury Grand Marquis, the pair made it to Amarillo, Texas, before a severe snowstorm forced them to spend three nights in the basement of a church. When the weather finally cleared, they went on to Phoenix.

Fat Sal may have been a rather odd choice to be asked along on a hit. His reputation was as a bank burglar and a master of electronic gadgetry. That made him valuable to the family as an earner, but he wasn't known as a killer.

However, he had a proven track record for being extremely resourceful. Sal had committed more than 30 bank burglaries from Brooklyn to South Carolina, usually by angling a homemade gaff and three-pronged spears into night-deposit boxes to pluck out the loot. For one Brooklyn heist, he rigged a remote-control drill to cut through concrete and steel. His organized-crime pals dubbed his capers "Fat Sallie Productions."

After an 18-month prison stretch in the mid-1990s for burglary, Mangiavillano was deported to Argentina, where he had original citizenship, but slipped across the Canadian border by negotiating his nearly 400-pound frame onto a Jet Ski for a ride across the Niagara River.

Back in Brooklyn in late 1999, while reuniting with his wife and three children, Sal got a call from Carbonaro, who pitched the idea of killing Gravano. Never much of an earner, Carbonaro had taken over Gravano's loansharking book, estimated to be worth more than $2 million, after Gravano flipped. But after a while, most refused to pay back a "rat's money" and the cash flow dried up.

However, according to prosecutors, what Carbonaro was good at was killing. During their cross-country trip, Carbonaro confided to Mangiavillano that the only person he regretted killing was his good friend Nicholas "Nicky Cowboy" Mormando, whom he murdered on Gravano's orders.

Carbonaro went to his bosses in 1999 to ask permission to kill Gravano, who, after leaving Witness Protection, suggested in a newspaper article that anyone foolish enough to come after him would be going home in a body bag.

"He [Gravano] was an embarrassment to them," Mangiavillano explained. "He was slapping them in the face."

If the hit was successful, Carbonaro would have been promoted to captain and Mangiavillano would have become a made man—a prospect that was not so enticing to Mangiavillano. As a made man, he'd be required to kick up money from his bank heists. Still, Sal felt he had little choice. If he refused, he probably would have been killed. "I couldn't tell him no," Mangiavillano said. "Once he asked me to go with him, I had to go with him."

After arriving in Phoenix, Carbonaro grew a beard and put hoop earrings in each ear. He took the name Henry Payne, which he thought sounded American. Mangiavillano chose Paul Milano.

They staked out the house on Secretariat Drive where Gravano's wife was living and considered hiding in a horse trailer to shoot him. Mangiavillano contemplated crafting a directional bomb that would shoot 12-gauge shotgun pellets. They also entertained sniping him from a spot behind his business. If they got too close, Mangiavillano feared, Gravano would kill them.

After a couple of reconnaissance missions, from New York to Arizona, the plot was ready to go. But in February 2000, when Mangiavillano was driving along FDR Drive, word came over the radio that Gravano had been arrested on drug-distribution charges.

"I had regrets that we didn't get to accomplish the mission after all the work we'd put in," Mangiavillano said.

Months later, Peter Gotti complained to associate Michael "Mikey Scars" DiLeonardo that he'd spent $70,000 on the Gravano hit and had no body to show for it. He questioned whether Carbonaro and Mangiavillano had actually made it to Arizona.

The FBI confirmed that they had. Over several months, Special Agent Theodore Otto retraced their route westward from Brooklyn to Phoenix. It all checked out, right down to the snowstorm in Amarillo.

Based in large part on Fat Sal's statements, federal prosecutors in Manhattan leveled new charges against Peter Gotti and Carbonaro, both of whom were already under an unrelated indictment in Brooklyn. And on December 22,

2004, on the strength of testimony from Mangiavillano, DiLeonardo, and two other mob turncoats, Gotti and Carbonaro were convicted of their roles in the plot to kill Gravano.

During his three days on the witness stand, Mangiavillano told jurors, "I pray to God at night that freedom comes."

A few days later, his prayers were answered. A Brooklyn judge released Mangiavillano from prison into the federal Witness Protection Program.

● ● ●

As 1999 came to a close Andrew was still incarcerated, but he too was beginning to see a flicker of light at the end of the tunnel. If he could win a reduced sentence for his parole violation, freedom might not be that far away.

21

2000

For Andrew the year 2000 started out with anticipation. He was sure the government was putting together additional cases that involved his past information and future testimony. But which cases were they? The government didn't disclose its intentions to witnesses until they felt the time was right. So guys like him were left to wait and wonder what was going to happen next.

While biding his time, Andrew also wondered when prosecutors would get around to charging Nicky Corozzo and Mike Yannotti in the murders of Robert Arena and Thomas Maranga, for which he'd provided them with information when he rolled in 1997. Going on three years later, he was still waiting to hear that arrests had been made or indictments issued.

Andrew was sure that from the time his cooperation with the government became public in 1998, Corozzo, Yannotti, and many others had been waiting for the law to knock on their door with an arrest warrant. And as the drug dealers and bank robbers were reeled in, the others had to know their turn was just a matter of time. So he probably wasn't the only one playing the anticipation game.

Nicky Corozzo and Mike Yannotti were his main interests, though. He had to give up the dealers and robbers in order to fulfill his agreement with the government. But Nick and Mike had been responsible for the death of his best friend. And that put them in a different category.

Corozzo was already in prison on racketeering charges unrelated to the Arena murder and wasn't scheduled for release until 2004. But Yannotti was still on the streets.

Andrew recalls what was going through his mind at the time.

"I was curious about what it was like for Mike. And every so often, I tried to put myself inside his head and the heads of some of my other former crew members who still had their freedom. They'd committed crimes with me and they knew how the government operated. Their witnesses were required to tell all they knew about everybody. They couldn't pick and choose who they gave up. With that knowledge, what was their stress level? I'm sure that as time passed and they weren't arrested, they tried to tell themselves that I'd held back and they weren't going down. On the other hand, they had to know that was just wishful thinking. They knew the knock would come. It was only a matter of time.

"The other thing I thought about a lot was my own freedom. My federal sentence expired in November. But I still had the state parole sentence to complete. As it stood, I was looking at an additional five years behind bars. If I could somehow get that sentence reduced I—or the new me—could be back on the streets much sooner than 2005.

"I was determined to pursue a sentence reduction and spent a lot of time doing research in the law library. I learned that the parole department held what they called 'reconsideration hearings' once a month throughout the state for selected cases. In order to get a hearing, the inmate had to file paperwork giving all the reasons he felt his sentence should be reduced. Although getting selected for a reconsideration hearing was a long shot, it was the only chance I had for an early release. I completed the application. But before I could send it out, I had what I like to call an intervention from above.

"It started when I was summoned to the case-manager's office for a legal call. It was Tom Scanlon, the state investigator who had arrested me on the fugitive warrant almost three years earlier. He got right to the point. The state needed my help in apprehending some people they wanted badly. Scanlon thought I could help them by providing some intelligence information based on my organized-crime history. So for the next few months, I helped him every chance I could.

"As with the feds, the state investigators gave no promises in return for my assistance. But I hoped that my extended cooperation would be taken into account when I finally submitted the reconsideration paperwork. Having them comment on the extent of my cooperation and the value of the information I provided could only be an asset in my dealings with the parole board.

"So as the summer passed, I was counting the days until everything would take place. I can only compare that time with waiting for a pot of water to boil. The more you watch, the longer it takes. But with the possibility that I could be a free man fairly soon, I had to get my things in order with my family. And if I did get out, I'd be entering phase two of the Witness Protection Program. Andrew DiDonato would cease to exist and some new person would take his place. I realized it would be a great opportunity to be rid of the criminal and all-around bad guy I'd been for most of my life. But the thought of being born again was a very scary prospect for me."

● ● ●

In early October, Andrew submitted his initial request for a special reconsideration hearing. Within weeks he received word that he'd get his hearing, but not until December. The fact that he would get a chance to present his case was great news. The only minor downside was that he would definitely remain locked up after the expiration of his federal sentence on November seventh. Although he felt he had a fair chance of getting a favorable decision, things could still go wrong.

Andrew went back to the torment of waiting for the water to come to a boil. In his idle moments, he thought about the upcoming hearing. What was the decision-making process of the parole board? Night after night he played devil's advocate, wondering how strong his presentation would really be. After all, just because they'd granted his request for a hearing didn't necessarily mean the board would side with him. Eventually, he had to force himself to stop thinking about it or risk driving himself crazy. The approaching Thanksgiving holiday helped serve as an escape from the mind games.

"I had to keep busy any way I could," Andrew recalls. "So two of my closest jailhouse friends and me started to prepare for Thanksgiving. By prepare, I mean we began stealing food from the mess hall two weeks out. We took a little bit at a time until we had enough for a feast. The crew we assembled to put on the meal consisted of me and three other Italian organized-crime guys. Two of us were from New York, the other two from Boston. We made it a point to feed as many of the other inmates as we could. But the four of us always came first.

"So as the days wound down to the holiday, the oldest of our group and our top chef, Mike, kept me busy stealing all the ingredients he thought we'd need for our Thanksgiving meal. Mike was also a Gambino guy who worked for a Bronx faction under the leadership of Frank [Frankie Loc] LoCascio. Mike was a sweetheart of a guy and turned out to be one of the best friends I'll ever have. Early on Thanksgiving morning, I went to the mess hall and stole a whole cooked turkey.

I hid it under my bed hoping that the other three birds they had would be enough to feed the fifty or so guys in the unit.

"As the main dinner was being served, one of the inmate workers dropped a whole turkey on the floor. To this day I believe he did it on purpose out of jealousy. They figured the dropped turkey would bring the missing bird to the attention of the civilian who ran the kitchen. Then he'd shake down the unit looking for it. But it was late in the day by then and the mess-hall boss wanted to get home to his family. So they started to serve chickens to supplement the turkeys.

"When the smoke cleared and everyone was busy doing other things, I brought the stolen bird into the dining area. I called about fifteen or so guys to eat with us to make up for anything they might have missed during the earlier dinner. I remember telling them that I knew some of them wanted to see us crash and burn, because they were jealous of us. I said my message to them was that they could go fuck themselves. In the future we wouldn't give them a fucking crumb.

"The meal was great. And later that night, Mike told us some good news for him. The day before he'd received his release papers. He'd be getting out just before Christmas. I was happy for him, but I knew my time would be harder to do without him. True friends are hard to come by and Mike was a true friend.

"In spite of Mike leaving, I was looking forward to December and my parole hearing. I knew things might not work out in my favor. But I had to get some kind of closure. Not knowing was worse than dealing with the result itself. And then I was notified that the hearing was postponed and rescheduled for February. As you can probably imagine, Christmas is stressful enough for guys in prison. Throwing in the uncertainty and frustration of the parole thing could have made me absolutely fuckin' miserable. But I refused to let it get to me.

"To keep my mind occupied, I planned and carried out

my annual Christmas food robbery from the mess hall, so the troops would have a good holiday. The heist went off without a hitch. Over my many years in prison, between working in the kitchen and preparing food in my cell, I'd become one hell of a cook. And those skills served me well in the years ahead.

"Even though I was keeping busy, I still thought about the parole situation sometimes. I began to wonder if the government was playing games behind the scenes and delaying the hearing. I hoped that wasn't true, but who the fuck knew?

"I called my ex-wife to let her know that there was a chance I'd get an early release and enter phase two of Witness Protection. I told her if that happened, I'd like to see my son before I was relocated. But Dina didn't want any part of it. We ended up in a good old-fashioned screaming match over the phone. She made it clear how much she hated me for my decision to roll and leaving them behind.

"That wasn't true, though. I gave them an opportunity to enter the program too. We wouldn't have been together while I was in prison, of course. But at least they'd have been safe. She chose door number two: to stay behind and remain friends with the Gambinos. And then she decided to turn her back on me altogether. She wouldn't even accept my phone calls.

"It had already been four years since I'd seen my son and under these circumstances, I knew it could be many more. I can't begin to tell you how that broke my heart. It's something I still carry with me today. I made many choices in my life that estranged me from Andrew Junior. They were mistakes and I hate myself for making them. But becoming a government witness was not one of them."

● ● ●

As 2000 came to a close, Andrew had good reason to experience feelings of anxiety. Was the government sabotaging his efforts for an early release? If and when he did get his hearing, what would the decision be? When would he be able to see his son again?

As the former gangster entered 2001, the future was anything but certain.

22
A New Beginning

In spite of the lingering doubts regarding his pending parole hearing, Andrew began 2001 with a positive attitude. He convinced himself that even if his bid for reconsideration failed, he was still way ahead of the game. He was, after all, a survivor. And compared to many of the situations he'd been confronted with over the years, doing another four years behind bars wouldn't be the end of the world.

But it turned out that his internal pep talks weren't really necessary. The same good fortune that had kept him from taking anyone's life during his numerous acts of violence smiled on him again. He recalls learning that he was going to be a free man after serving only half of his parole-violation sentence.

"I called home one night in January to speak with my mother. As soon as she answered the phone, I could hear the excitement in her voice. She was bursting at the seams to give me the good news. She'd received a call from my case agent saying that the parole board had reviewed my case and voted to grant me an immediate release. I was in shock. I didn't even know my case was being reviewed. I was under the impression nothing would happen on my case until the hearing scheduled for February.

"I remember being too emotional to speak right away. I

don't know if those who have never lost their freedom and then regained it can appreciate what it was like to hear that news. But I'm sure that any guys reading this who were ever incarcerated know exactly what I'm talking about when I say how emotional it was. It's a feeling that goes beyond happiness.

"But there was a scary side to it as well. My whole life was about to change. I'd spent many nights in my cell staring at the ceiling and planning for my release. But now that it was almost a reality, I realized that I was far from being prepared. I wouldn't be back on the streets of Brooklyn where I knew my way around. In fact, I'd probably never be in my old neighborhood again. There would be no more crime and no more big scores and no more easy money. That had been Andrew DiDonato's thing and he'd be gone. The new me would hit the streets as a legitimate citizen and I'd have to play by the same rules as everybody else. I'd have to go to work and pay my bills.

"For most of my life, I'd faced dangerous scenarios and stress that might have brought down a two-ton elephant. And there I was thinking about having to get a real job and it scared the hell out of me. It might not make sense to most people, but I was terrified.

"But I knew I couldn't let that fear get the best of me. I was getting a new chance at life and I wasn't going to blow it by going back to my old ways. I'd have to succeed at whatever real job I got. If I didn't, I could easily end up going back to making money the only way I'd ever known. And I wasn't going to let that happen. When the gates opened for me, failure would not be an option. I was committed to becoming a regular guy.

"With no formal training or experience in the real world and no background information to put on a job application, I knew it wouldn't be easy. But if I could survive the streets of New York and deal with some of the most ruthless criminals in the country, I knew I could handle being a working stiff in the real America.

"Not being able to have personal contact with my family was another matter. I knew that would be much harder on me than leading a legitimate life. Yeah, that would be tough. But I was going to be an active witness against some bad people and my family didn't need me around to expose them to any danger. Their safety was worth any sacrifice I had to make."

● ● ●

On April 6, 2001, Andrew was again a free man. Well, kind of. He was no longer Andrew DiDonato. And as a participant in the Witness Protection Program, the feds were keeping an eye on him. When the gate closed behind him that day, he entered a whole new world. Andrew explains what it was like.

"Learning the rules and how to interact with the Marshals Service was quite a shock to me, a guy who'd never been controlled like that before. After that I had to go through a cleansing period where I was given a new identity. And then it was time to get back into society and show the world that I was capable of being an honest productive citizen. It took me about a month to get up and running.

"I secured a driver's license and bought a car. And then came the job hunt. I read every available newspaper in search of a way for a person in my position to earn money without drawing attention. When I wasn't reading the paper, I was out pounding the pavement looking for my ideal job. I tried real hard, but I wasn't able to find what I was looking for, what I'd be comfortable with.

"I finally came to the conclusion that I should open my own business. That would eliminate having to pass the scrutiny of potential employers who would be skeptical of hiring a thirty-five-year-old man with no work history or references. The only obstacle was money.

"I didn't have unlimited financial resources available to me any longer. In my previous life, I always had a stash I could go to when needed. But those days were gone. I was now Joe Citizen dropped from the fuckin' sky to the Midwest with no history or money. I still didn't let that stop me. After some intense thought, I came up with what I thought to be the monster plan. I'd always loved to cook and that was the one thing I could do that was legitimate. So I decided to open a pizza restaurant.

"Like a sign from above, the very next day I saw an ad in the paper for a restaurant for sale. When I called to get the information, the guy on the other end of the line offered to practically give me the place. It turned out he was a real estate-agent who owned the restaurant and several other properties. He wasn't interested in the business at all. His previous tenant had walked out and left everything. He wanted to either sell the building or have someone take over the lease. So we made a great deal that benefited both of us. I signed a lease to take over the business and would make monthly payments to purchase the equipment.

"When I think back on it now, it's kind of funny. There I was in parts unknown trying to bring the flavor of Italy to these people who thought Olive Garden is gourmet Italian food. It was interesting, to say the least. Almost as soon as I opened the shop, business started booming. I knew I was a good cook. But not good enough to account for the lines of customers I was getting. And then it hit me like a shot. It wasn't just my cookin' that was bringing people in. They were coming to see the show. I was like a circus act. My accent and sense of humor drew them like flies.

"All day long I'd hear, 'I love your accent. You're not from here. I bet you're from New York.' My response was always the same. I'd smile and say I knew it wasn't my accent that gave me away, it was my complexion. The customers always burst out laughing like it was the funniest line they'd ever heard. I didn't care what they thought. I was making great money. And it was all legal."

But over time, some of the locals became suspicious of the stranger. Who was he, really? What brought him to their town? What did he do before he came there? When Andrew failed to satisfy their curiosity, some people provided their own answers. Maybe he was really a drug dealer. Or perhaps the pizza joint was being used to launder money for the Mob. The rumors swirled. Andrew wasn't bothered by them, though. In fact, he thought they were funny.

Although he was suspected by some of being involved in criminal activity, he hadn't reverted to that part of his past life. However, the new Andrew had retained the temper of the old one. And he put that emotion on display one afternoon when his eatery was filled with customers.

"A lady called to order a pineapple pizza. I explained to her that we used only authentic Italian toppings and pineapple wasn't one of them. I told her the options. She picked one and my driver delivered it. A while later, her husband walked in with the pizza box and slammed it on the counter. He looked like a real farmer trying to play tough guy. He told my counter man that the pizza wasn't what his wife wanted to order. She'd been forced into taking something else and he wanted his money back.

"I walked over to him and said, 'Listen to me and listen good. Don't come into my place barkin' orders and actin' tough. If you say one more word, I'm gonna put your fuckin' head in that oven. Here's your ten bucks. Now get the hell out while you still can. And don't come back.' He backed out the door and I never saw him again.

"After he left, you could have heard a pin drop in the place. I glanced around and every eye was on me. I told them the show was over and to get back to their food. They immediately started looking at their plates."

Such incidents were the exception. For the most part Andrew had a lot of fun running the restaurant. And he made some good money. He lived alone in a nice three-bedroom apartment and was able to buy a brand new Cadillac.

Even though he was enjoying himself and making money, Andrew just wasn't a small-town guy. He found living in a Mayberry-like community to be a bit suffocating. It was only a matter of time before he moved on. The following year, citing a drop in business, he relocated to a more heavily populated area.

Although Andrew had failed to take root in his first attempt, he did accomplish a very important thing. He proved to himself that he could be successful in a legitimate business. And he also proved it to those who had predicted he would return to a life of crime before the ink on his parole papers had dried. The fears he'd experienced before being released from prison were gone, replaced by a growing confidence. He didn't need to have a gun in his belt to survive. He was at peace with himself.

While Andrew was experiencing peace, some of his former associates were feeling something else: heat. For them, the chickens were coming home to roost. The next several months wouldn't be good ones for Nicky Corozzo and his pals.

A Court Date Nears

After leaving the Midwest, Andrew took up residence in the Northwest. His new location was more densely populated and he enjoyed the hustle and bustle that reminded him of his days on the streets of New York City.

After settling in, Andrew continued his self-employment. He bought a delivery truck from the profits of his pizza restaurant and became an independent driver for a major bread distributor. He worked the graveyard shift and was home by seven o'clock most mornings. For the most part, he was his own boss and the money was good.

But it wasn't long before the distributor began calling during the day to have accounts replenished or make sales calls on potential customers. Andrew worked on a percentage basis of sales and didn't feel these extra hours did much to increase his checks. In his opinion, the distributor was the only one to really benefit.

"Here's an example," Andrew says. "I'd been home about two hours after working a ten-hour shift. I was just getting to sleep when the bakery called. They wanted me to come back in to deliver ten loaves of bread to a store downtown. Do the math. That was about a twelve-dollar order and I only got a percentage of it. In addition to the time involved, there was the cost of fuel to run the truck back and forth. So a run like that would have taken me a couple of hours and ten bucks or so in gas to make two dollars and forty cents.

"When I started getting calls like that on a regular basis, I knew this wasn't the right business for me. This guy was a millionaire and I could understand why. He was an arrogant bastard and he thought because he gave me a paycheck, he was entitled access to me any time of the day or night. If I'd have run into him a few years earlier, I'd have found a way to shake him down. But I was a gentleman. I told him I needed to move on and asked him to buy my truck. I sold it to him the next day."

After quitting the bread route, Andrew turned to something he was more familiar with. He opened an Italian deli and restaurant. He was back in his element.

"The concept was great. And a large Italian population from back east was eager for the Italian delicacies I offered. But my place was in a new mall with a lot of spaces that hadn't been rented yet. That meant almost no foot traffic or other businesses to draw customers from. After about a year and a half, I had to give it up."

From time to time, Andrew read or heard news about some of his former acquaintances. The first of them to come to his attention was a newspaper report that his friend and fellow Gambino man Sal Mangiavillano had become a government witness.

"Fat Sal and me had been friends since I was about seventeen years old," Andrew said. "And later on in my criminal career when I was on the run, Sal and his crew took me in and helped me earn. He was a true friend and a mentor to me. Sal was a prolific bank robber and opened my eyes to a lot of things. I ended up having closer friendships with Sal and his guys than I did with my own Corozzo crew.

"The article told how Sal had been mistreated by the Gambinos just like I had. He'd been sent to Arizona by Peter Gotti to kill Sammy Gravano. The hit never came off and when Sal got back to New York, he was arrested and locked up on other charges. For two years, nobody from the Gambinos paid any attention to him. And then when word got out that the feds were looking to indict some people for the plot against Gravano, the boys suddenly remembered Sal.

"The bastards wanted to keep Sal on the reservation, so they sent him a letter saying they were thinking of him. And with the letter was a check for fifty dollars. Fifty fuckin' dollars! These goddamn millionaires had the balls to send Sal fifty bucks to keep his mouth shut. It didn't work. Sal flipped and gave up the whole Gravano deal. I was glad to see he'd done the right thing. And again, the guys who went down only had to look in the mirror to see who was to blame.

"The way they handled me, Sal, and a lot of others is the reason the Mob is in the shape it is today. You can't treat your people like shit and expect them to take it on the chin for you. Loyalty has to work both ways. The current bosses in the American Mafia don't understand that. They take the guys on the street for granted. To them, guys like Sal and me are expendable. But they're finding out that we can fight back. And as far as I'm concerned, they're getting what they deserve."

● ● ●

While Andrew was adapting to his new life and hearing news about some of his former friends and associates, the wheels of justice were moving slowly forward.

In March 2004, Nicky Corozzo made the news. Just months away from his scheduled release from prison on his 1996 racketeering indictment and subsequent conviction, the word circulated that the feds had come up with information tying him to the 1992 shooting of Guardian Angels founder Curtis Sliwa and two unsolved gangland murders.

According to published reports, in April 1996 FBI agents had heard Corozzo admit to a wired informant that in 1985, he'd feared for his life after John Gotti took control of the Gambinos from the slain Paul Castellano. But in late 1996, as the Dapper Don languished in prison and his appeals were exhausted, Nick was tapped by family capos to replace Gotti as the boss. His reign lasted only a matter of days and came to an end with his arrest in Florida and incarceration on the racketeering indictment. To the government, Nick was the kind of guy they would just as soon keep behind bars if they could.

Corozzo's pending legal problems reportedly dated back to 1992, when he became a confidant of John Gotti, Jr., who had assumed the role of acting head of the family following his father's conviction and life sentence.

Government prosecutors allegedly had information that Nick had assisted the younger Gotti in his plan to kill Sliwa by providing the triggerman, Mike Yannotti, to carry out the hit. The feds also believed that in January 1996, Yannotti gunned down two men on a Brooklyn street over a drug dispute and that Nick Corozzo authorized the killings. The two dead men were Andrew's friend Robert Arena and Thomas Maranga.

Corozzo's attorney responded to the reports by denying that his client had anything to do with drugs or the murders.

But it turned out that the government wasn't ready to move against Nick Corozzo at that time. He was released from prison in June and returned to the position of capo in the Gambino family.

● ● ●

In July 2004, John Gotti, Jr. and three others were indicted on racketeering charges. The underlying crimes included murder, attempted murder, conspiracy to commit murder, kidnapping, and conspiracy to commit kidnapping, conspiracy to commit securities fraud, mail fraud, wire fraud, extortion, and illegal gambling. The kidnapping and attempted murder allegations had to do with the 1992 attack on Curtis Sliwa.

Gotti's co-defendants were alleged Gambino crime-family soldiers Joseph "Little Joey" D'Angelo and Michael "Mikey Y" Yannotti and family associate Louis "Louie Black" Mariani.

Andrew followed these stories with great interest. Cases were moving forward and he would most likely have to appear in court as a government witness in the not-too-distant future.

24

The Junior Gotti and Mike Yannotti Trial

On August 8, 2005, the trial of John Gotti, Jr., and Mike Yannotti began in U.S. District Court in Manhattan with Judge Shira Scheindlin presiding. In his opening statement, Gotti's lawyer, Jeffrey Lichtman, made clear what he thought of several of the names on the government's witness list. He described them as turncoats and violent manipulative creeps. One of the witnesses he was referring to was Andrew DiDonato.

Andrew was flown back to New York and took the stand on August 11. For the first time in years, he would be eyeball to eyeball with Mike Yannotti. It was a time he'll never forget.

"The day I landed in New York, I was immediately taken to the United States Attorney's office where I met with prosecutors. They informed me I'd be called to testify in a matter of hours. Needless to say, I was immediately tense. I knew my testimony would take many hours—I was actually on the stand for three days—and those hours would feel like an eternity. My whole life was going to be an open book for the world to see. My entire criminal history would be put under the microscope for the defense attorneys to pick apart like vultures.

"When I entered the courtroom for the first time, it was dead quiet. After being sworn in, I sat in the witness chair and was face to face with Junior Gotti and Mike Yannotti. It had been a long time since me and Mike had been that close. Our eyes locked on each other and I sensed he held a glimmer of hope that I would remember all those years we were in the trenches together and find a way to hold back what I knew—to spare him. But it was much too late for that. And as I looked at Junior, it wasn't hope that I saw in his eyes. It was fear.

"The entire first day I spent on the stand was under direct questioning from the prosecutor. We pretty much touched on my entire crime history, my relationships within the Gambino family, and my crimes with Yannotti and the Corozzo crew. That day opened up many old wounds. As the prosecutor walked me down memory lane, he brought out all the devastation I had caused over the years, the harm I'd done for my own personal gain, and for the benefit of the Gambino crime family.

"As I recounted crime after crime, I saw Mike squirming in his chair like a school kid waiting for the recess bell to ring so he could run from the classroom. As for me, for a long time I'd wondered if I'd really be able to testify when the time came. Would I be able to tell it all honestly and coherently? Or would I stumble and come across as a liar or an idiot? But any doubts passed quickly and I found no hesitation in my answers. I think knowing that I was doing the right thing kept my words flowing smoothly.

"I was called upon to listen to a number of audiotapes the government had acquired during their investigation. On them Mike discussed his involvement in the loanshark business. The prosecutor had me explain in layman's terms what Mike meant when he used certain words and phrases. The defense objected to that testimony, but the judge allowed it. It wasn't real exciting stuff, like doing murder. But I felt at the time those tapes and my explanation would lead to Mike's downfall.

"I truly believe that a mobster and the truth cannot share the same space. With each word that came from my mouth, I could see Mike becoming more and more uncomfortable, especially when I dropped the bombshell of my knowledge of the deaths of Robert Arena and Thomas Maranga. I also gave testimony about another homicide—Todd Alvino—that sent the defense team reeling and shouting objections. They were upset because the Alvino killing was not part of the original indictment and it would spell even more trouble for Mike.

"With so much on the table, the judge immediately had the jury removed from the courtroom, so I could be questioned in more detail about the new homicide. After ten minutes, it was perfectly clear to everyone in the room that my knowledge and deep involvement in the Alvino thing was real. But the judge ended up ruling that the prejudicial effect of that testimony was too great and wouldn't allow it in. But she said her decision didn't mean it couldn't be used in a future case. I believe in my heart that Mike thinks about that every day of his life. Knowing that someday him and me might be back in court again with me on the witness stand and him at the defense table.

"After hours of direct testimony, much of which was objected to by the defense, it was clear that my information had done a couple of very important things for the government. It established that the Gambino crime family was an organization—a corrupt organization. It had structure and a chain of command. It made money from the criminal activities of its members.

"It also exposed Mike's involvement in many crimes, including shaking down drug dealers and shylocking. Many of those crimes I had been directly involved in and others I had knowledge of. And it left no doubt that most, if not all, of our criminal acts were for the sole purpose of trying to advance ourselves within the ranks of the Gambino crime family. The basis for the racketeering charges against Mike was set.

"As these things played out in the courtroom, I kept a cool head, knowing that this was only the direct testimony and things would start really heating up the next day when the defense tried to discredit me and my testimony."

Andrew's concerns were well-founded. When the defense got their chance at him, they attacked with a vengeance.

"Now it was the defense's turn to try and get Mike out from under the damage my testimony had done," Andrew recalls. "Mike's chief lawyer was Diamuid White. But White didn't cross-examine me; they had another guy do that. He started out the way I figured he would, pointing out to the jury my life of crime and all the despicable things I'd done over the years. How could anyone believe me today?

"And when he asked that question I said, 'Yes. I lied, cheated, scammed, and plotted every day of my adult life, because that's what organized crime is. It's a never-ending lie that exploits every citizen with whom it comes in contact. So yes, I am guilty of it all. But I'm no longer that person.'

"And then I said something to the effect that if I was in court to lie, I'd be sitting at the defense table with him or one of his colleagues representing me. I told him that my record was an open book. I wasn't proud of it. But at least all my cards were on the table. I wasn't hiding behind a lawyer trying to profess my innocence.

"I don't think this attorney realized that the worse he made me look, the worse he was making his client look as well. Like the old saying says, birds of a feather flock together. If I was that bad, what did it make Mike?

"But I think the defense team was desperate and felt their only chance was to make me the villain. So the lawyer kept up his verbal assault, trying to trip me up at every turn. I'd implicated Mike in four Mob-related shootings, three of which ended in homicide. And as questions came my way about each act, I truly believe Mike's lawyer was hurting him, not helping him. He seemed to constantly get the names of the victims wrong. And I think to confuse me, he sometimes put a name to a different crime. But in my opinion, that only made him seem unprepared. I think the deeper he got into those subjects, the more credibility he gave me.

"And then the defense turned their attention to Junior Gotti. What if any business dealings had I had with him? I made it clear to the court and jury that I'd met him at Gambino social events on several occasions over the years, but I'd never had any personal dealings with him. When asked what status Gotti held in the family, I explained that after his father went to prison, he sat on the panel of family leaders with Nicky Corozzo and Jackie D'Amico.

"When they challenged my statement, I explained that I knew about the leadership panel from conversations with Nicky Corozzo and from being part of Nicky's crew. Crew members have to know who their leaders are; it's a part of their survival. It's like working for a major corporation. The average employees may not speak with board members directly, but they know who they are.

"Junior's story was that he'd walked away from the Mob years earlier. I disputed that. So they came at me hard, wanting me to explain how I could say that it's impossible for a made member, boss or soldier, to walk away from the life. I answered that for many years, I was schooled in the rules of the life by Nicky Corozzo. I also told about the time I tried to get released from the Gambino family to join the Colombos. Nicky read me the riot act by saying in no uncertain terms that I was born under the Gambino flag and that's where I would die.

"When asked what knowledge I had of any business dealings between Junior and Nicky, I stated they were involved in a long-distance phone-card business. Of course, the lawyer asked if it was an illegal business and that I had to answer yes or no. Because of that I answered no, it wasn't illegal. What I wasn't allowed to say was that while the business itself was legal, their business practices weren't. Not when guys like me went to the merchants and told them they could only sell that particular card or else. So the defense got away with one.

"But I was able to get in Nicky's plot to kill Junior because he felt he was being cheated on his end of the phone-card business. Because me and Mike were supposed to do the work, I can imagine the co-defendant meetings between Junior and Mike got a little tense after that came out.

"Moments like that reveal the level of treachery behind the scenes. On the surface, it looked like those two guys were allies against the justice system. But in reality, either one of them would have killed the other if ordered.

"For the two days I was under cross-examination, I was called a murderer, a liar, and a cheat. But they really showed how much they felt they needed to neutralize me when they accused me of beating Dina when she was nine months pregnant. How was that for a desperate effort to get jurors to look at me with disgust? But they failed to do their homework, because during Dina's ninth month of pregnancy, I was on the run and had no contact with her.

"It's things like that guys like me who turn government witness can expect from defense lawyers. If the government takes you on as a witness, it's because they believe you can help drive a nail into somebody's coffin. One way to overcome damaging testimony is to make the witness seem even more despicable to the jury than the defendant. Lies and slanderous accusations are the Mob's only defense against the truth.

"Mike's lawyers went as far as trying to blame me and two other Gambino soldiers for the murders of Robert Arena and Thomas Maranga. I wonder if those guys were happy with Mike's decision to implicate them in a double homicide just to save his own ass. Was that an example of the idealistic

Mob rules we hear about? No, it was not. But it does illustrate the big lie that the Mob of today is built on.

"For the record, it should be known that testifying brought me no pleasure, only sadness. I thought Mike was throwing his life away to appease and protect those in power who didn't give a rat's ass about guys like him or me. But it was his decision and he'd have to live with it.

"When my testimony was over, I left the stand knowing I'd done what I had to do. But I was glad it was over."

The jury got the case on September 8. On September 20, the judge declared a mistrial in the case against Junior Gotti. Michael Yannotti was convicted on only one count: racketeering conspiracy based on the extortion and loansharking aspects of the racketeering charges. And these were the allegations that Andrew addressed in great detail during his testimony, over the strenuous objections of Yannotti's lawyer.

YANNOTTI TAKES IN SOME MONEY ...

On January 26, 2006, an article appeared in the *Gang Land News* relating to a rather odd fundraiser that had been held a couple of weeks earlier. The event was a well-attended $1,000-a-plate dinner to help pay the legal fees the incarcerated Mike Yannotti accumulated during his 2005 racketeering trial. Sources told *Gang Land* that between $250,000 and $400,000 was raised.

It was reported that more than 300 of Yannotti's friends and associates showed up to demonstrate their support for the alleged gangster. For their donations, the attendees were treated to a buffet, beer, and wine, but no hard liquor. Nicky Corozzo was listed as a no-show.

Although Nicky wasn't at the event, Andrew believes he was the catalyst behind it.

"I think the fundraiser was orchestrated by Nicky and was more or less a shakedown. He probably put the word out that everyone was expected to attend the event and nobody dared to not show up. Don't forget that Mike no doubt had enough on Nicky to bury him if he ever flipped. Raising money for Mike's legal fees would have been a good move on Nicky's part."

... BUT LOSES BIG

In November 2006, Yannotti appeared before Judge Shira Scheindlin for sentencing. Probation officials anticipated he'd get four years of prison time. However, to the surprise of many, Scheindlin slapped Mikey Y with the maximum allowable sentence of 20 years.

Prosecutors had argued that she should consider the attempted murder of Curtis Sliwa when deciding on Yannotti's punishment. Even though he was acquitted of the charge, the government contended that ample proof of his guilt had been presented. A number of observers concluded that the judge agreed with the prosecution's argument. But that wasn't the only hit the convict suffered at the hands of the legal system.

Following his conviction, Yannotti filed an appeal. One of his complaints was that Andrew's testimony at trial was inappropriately allowed into evidence. The United States Court of Appeals for the Second Circuit heard the case in August 2007. The decision was rendered in September 2008.

Per Federal Rules of Evidence 701, three conditions must be met in order to allow lay testimony into evidence: It must be rationally based on the perception of the witness, helpful to a clear understanding of the witness' testimony or the determination of a fact in issue, and not based on scientific, technical, or other specialized knowledge.

The Court ruled that Andrew's testimony met all three of those conditions and the decision by the trial court to allow his testimony was affirmed.

25

Closing in on Nicky

February 2008 was not a good month for Nicky Corozzo. He was one of 26 people indicted in Queens County, resulting from a multi-year investigation called Operation Touchback. The 29 counts in the indictment focused primarily on illegal gambling. At the same time, the feds announced that Nicky was also named in the indictment arising from their Operation Old Bridge investigation. Old Bridge was massive in scope, involving the FBI and police in Italy. The federal allegations included myriad racketeering charges, the murders of Robert Arena and Thomas Maranga among them.

The February 7th Queens County indictment was particularly interesting, because it detailed the Gambino gambling setup, much of which involved online betting. It appeared Nicky and his boys had gone high-tech.

The indictment was on charges of operating highly sophisticated illegal-gambling enterprises in Queens County and elsewhere that booked nearly $10 million in wagers over a two-year period on professional and college basketball and football, professional baseball and hockey, and other sporting events. Twenty of the defendants were in custody and six were being sought. Nicky Corozzo was one of the latter six.

The defendants were alleged to have gone online, supplementing traditional wire-room and street-corner bookie operations with offshore-based Internet websites designed for sports betting and casino-style gambling. Toll-free telephone numbers were established, through which numerous gambling accounts were managed and out of which criminal proceeds were collected and distributed throughout the New York City metropolitan area. The computerized wire rooms operated around the clock and handled a large volume of bettors at any one time, allowing the defendants to increase their illicit profits without having to bother with the time-consuming record-keeping aspects of a more traditional paper-based bookmaking operation. The Gambino crime family allegedly took in millions of dollars each year through the illegal gambling scheme.

The defendants were charged with enterprise corruption—a violation of New York State's Organized Crime Control Act—as well as promoting gambling, criminal usury, grand larceny, and conspiracy. They faced up to 25 years in prison if convicted.

The specifics of the indictment filed in Queens County Supreme Court alleged that the gambling ring promoted illegal sports betting in Queens County and elsewhere and that the defendants were involved in traditional gambling wire rooms located at 85-50 Forest Parkway in Woodhaven, as well as nontraditional computerized wire rooms in Costa Rica.

Six of the defendants were also being sued civilly and named as respondents in a $9.8 million civil-forfeiture action filed in Queens Supreme Court by the District Attorney's Special Proceedings Bureau, which alleged that they engaged in a criminal enterprise that promoted illegal-gambling activities and generated illegal wages.

The criminal enterprise was generally known as the "Nicky Corozzo Crew of the Gambino Crime Family" and allegedly handled thousands of wagers each month that generated hundreds of thousands of dollars in monthly gross revenue, or approximately $9.8 million between November 6, 2005, and January 8, 2008.

Authorities believed the operation relied on modern technology, including toll-free telephone numbers and four known gambling websites, BETMSG.com; BETALLSPORTS.com; BETWSI.com; and BETOFFSHORE.net, which served as computerized wire rooms through which the enterprise conducted much of its illegal gambling activity. Account information was typically stored on computer servers outside the United States—often in such Central American countries as Costa Rica—which "bounced" their data through a series of server nodes in efforts to evade law-enforcement detection through traditional methods.

According to the indictment, Nicholas Corozzo was the boss of the enterprise. He controlled and oversaw the entire operation and profited from each criminal pursuit by the other members. Corozzo was also alleged to have benefited from a prostitution ring to the tune of $500 per week.

Nick was in big trouble. When his daughter tipped him off that the law was scooping up his co-defendants, he did what Andrew had done 12 years earlier. He went on the lam.

AMW JOINS THE MANHUNT

On May 17, just over three months after Nicky went on the run, "America's Most Wanted" profiled him on its TV show. Its report recapped his criminal history and the pending charges. The heat was on Nick big time.

And "AMW" cameras were on hand 12 days later when, with his lawyer by his side, an exhausted-looking Nicky Corozzo surrendered to authorities on a street corner outside the FBI's office in lower Manhattan. At his arraignment, Nicky pled guilty to all charges and was ordered held without bail.

VINDICATION

On August 14, 2008, Nick Corozzo avoided a jury trial by pleading guilty to ordering the January 26, 1996, murder of Robert Arena, which also resulted in the death of Thomas Maranga. Andrew was on an airplane on the way to testify against Nick when the deal was made.

"It happened while I was in flight," Andrew remembers. "When I landed, I was told that Nicky's defense team had worked out a deal with the U.S. Attorney. Nicky pled guilty to being part of the conspiracy to murder Robert and Thomas. Hearing that was music to my ears. After so many years of being called a liar and all the denials by Nicky and his attorneys, I was finally vindicated. And he had been exposed for the liar he is."

THE ACCOUNTING

On April 17, 2009, Nicky Corozzo was sentenced to 13½ years in federal prison for his role in the Arena and Maranga murders.

In July 2008, he had pled guilty to the state enterprise corruption charges. On April 28, 2009, he was sentenced to a prison term of 4½ to 13½ years on those charges.

Corozzo is serving the sentences concurrently at a federal correctional facility. His projected release date is March 2, 2020, two weeks before his 80th birthday.

26 Lessons

When Andrew and I began writing this book, he was emphatic about one of the things he wanted to accomplish. His primary goal was to get the word out to young men, who might be considering a life of crime, that they'd be making a very bad mistake. He hoped that learning what he'd gone through would cause them to think twice before going down that road.

In closing, he wants to reiterate in his own words the lessons he learned while living the life. And he hopes those lessons will discourage others from following in his footsteps.

● ● ●

"Being an organized-crime guy is for losers. I say that based on my own experience. When I got into the life, I was excited. I thought I was part of something—a family that took care of its own. Everybody looked out for each other and nobody would dare fuck with us. That's what I thought. I was wrong.

"For fifteen years, I was a predator. Everybody was a potential victim to me. From the time I got up in the morning until I went to sleep at night, I planned, plotted, and schemed how I could take advantage of people. If I could get their money through fraud, I would. If I could get it through robbery or burglary, I would. And if I could get it through violence or the threat of violence, I would.

"I made a lot of money during those years. I also made a lot of money for my boss, Nicky Corozzo, and the Gambino crime family. To make that money, I hurt an awful lot of people. They weren't all victims of my crimes either. Some of them were the people who cared about me the most, who loved me. But I didn't think about that then. I hurt virtually everyone I came in contact with physically, financially, or emotionally.

"Do you know what I ended up with when it all came crashing down? Nothing. I didn't have a goddamn dime. Nicky and some lawyers did okay on me. But it turned out that I hurt all those people for nothing. When the end came I was broke, facing decades in prison and under a death sentence from a couple of organized-crime families. A real success story, huh?

"If that isn't a turn-off, try this. When I was still in the life, but having second thoughts, my father wanted to make a point. He asked me to write down my ten closest friends in the life. After I did that, he told me to write what each one was doing then. Out of the ten, six were in prison and four were dead. I guess you could call that a one hundred percent failure rate.

"With all those bad things I did, there was one decision I made that I know was right. When I got the green light to kill my brother-in-law, when I held the power of life and death over him, I let him live. My niece has a father and that's the way it should be. So that was one choice that I'll never regret making.

"That aside, I'm alive and free. So what am I complaining about, you ask? First, I'm not complaining. I'm stating facts. And having my life and freedom carries costs that can't be ignored. I was born Andrew DiDonato and he no longer exists. I haven't seen my son or family in years and don't know if or when I'll see them again. Yes, I'm alive. But there's a big hole inside of me.

"I'm alive because I was lucky—very lucky. I was shot at a few times by guys with bad aims. And I got into Witness Protection before my former colleagues could get me. If not for that good fortune—or divine intervention—we wouldn't be having this conversation.

"And I owe my freedom to luck or fate too. I shot several people, but none of them died. I shot Ralph Burzo in the head and the bullet struck a bone and splintered. When I was going to finish him off, Sandra Raiola was there staring at me, so I couldn't. Somebody was watching over Burzo or me. Either way, it turned out to be a blessing.

"When Mike Yannotti failed to kill Sammy Karkis, I was pissed off. But Nicky actually did me a favor by stopping the hit. If it had gone through, there's a good chance I could have been charged with conspiracy to commit murder and I might still be locked up. And by the time I was in a position to kill Sammy myself, I had come to realize that his death would have been an injustice. He wasn't in the life and yet I had expected him to play by my rules. Sammy didn't put me in prison. I put myself there. He wasn't to blame and didn't deserve to die. I know that he has a young daughter now. Someday he'll walk her down the aisle at her wedding, and I feel good about that.

"When I look back at it, I realize how many times I came close to becoming a murderer. And each time a matter of inches—or with Burzo a fraction of an inch—resulted in my victim's wounds being non-fatal.

"And it wasn't just the shootings. In 1984 when we blew up the cars in the garage of that house Vic Amuso's nephew was staying in, nobody inside got killed. What about the night I was driving the Mercedes shell and being chased by the cops? I ran every traffic light and made it through all those intersections doing over a hundred miles an hour and nobody died or even got hurt. But if they had—especially some innocent motorists—I'd have been responsible.

"So yeah, I was damn lucky. I know it and I thank God for it every day.

"If you think joining the Mob means you're entering a life of honor, you'd better think again. It ain't like what you might see on television or in the movies. That's right, in today's Mob, that old saying about honor among thieves is a lot of bullshit, trust me.

"Let's take the leadership. When I was a kid, I thought the bosses walked on water. They were legends in the neighborhood. But when I was in prison, several of them were in there with me. I even shared a cell with a couple. I'm telling you straight that most of the Mob icons I met behind bars didn't match their street reputations. When it came to winning their criminal cases, they were willing to throw anybody and everybody under the bus to beat the rap. Real standup guys.

"It's very important that you understand this. In today's Mob, the money and loyalty go from the bottom up. They don't come back down to the guys on the street. If you get pinched and have to do some time, don't count on your crime family to take care of your real family.

"Look what they did to Fat Sal. He was loyal and one hell of an earner. They forgot about him for two years while he was locked up. And then when they were worried about Sal flipping, they sent him fifty fuckin' bucks for his commissary! He kicked a lot of money up to these guys and that's how they thanked him. That shows the definition of loyalty from the bosses' perspective.

"So if you take the organized-crime route, the people you'll be associating with won't be true friends. The bosses will use you to make themselves rich and do their dirty work. They'll pick your bones clean. And in the life you're only as good as your last earn. So if you stop producing, you'll become expendable.

"You'll also be in jeopardy if you become too good at your job. If the boss thinks you've become a threat to him, that you have designs on his job and the ability to do it, you're probably not long for this world.

"And if you fall out of favor with your boss and have to go, one or more of your peers will likely be assigned to eliminate you. The guy you've committed crimes and socialized with for years will have dinner with you one night and put a couple in your head the next.

"I'm currently doing organized-crime-related volunteer work. I help law-enforcement agencies by educating their investigators on how the Mob operates. I also counsel at-risk youths who are at a crossroads in their lives. I tell them the same things I'm telling you here.

"There is no honor or glory in being a gangster and the retirement options suck. If you want to dance at your daughter's wedding or be at the ceremony when your grandson graduates from high school, you'd better choose another line of work.

"I know that many of you I'm trying to reach will think I'm full of shit. You know better, right? The crew you'll hook up with won't have any Nicky Corozzos or Mike Yannottis. Even if it does, you're too smart and tough to be taken advantage of. If you believe that, I've got a bridge in Brooklyn I'd like to sell you. The only trouble is I can't go back there to sign the papers.

"Seriously though, one time when my father visited me while I was in state prison, he said there are only two options for organized-crime guys: prison or death on the street. He asked me why I thought I'd be the exception to the rule. I didn't answer him, but in my mind I thought I was too smart and tough to end up back behind bars or dead. Yeah, right.

"Jail cells, cemeteries, landfills, and sometimes the trunks of abandoned cars usually end up as the homes of guys who thought they were too smart and tough. I wasn't, they weren't, and you aren't. The life is like making a deal with the devil. Don't do it.

"Having said all that, I don't know how many of you wannabe wiseguys will have second thoughts. But let me be perfectly clear. If even one young man—just one—is willing to accept the truth and change the course he's on, I will have made a difference."

Index

                 Surviving the Mob

ABOUT HUNTINGTON PRESS

Huntington Press is a specialty publisher of Las
Vegas- and gambling-related books and periodicals,
including the award-winning consumer newsletter,
Anthony Curtis' Las Vegas Advisor.

Huntington Press
3665 Procyon Street
Las Vegas, Nevada 89103